Janis

Omega Cometh

Omega Cometh

James R. Spillman

Fleming H. Revell Company
Old Tappan, New Jersey

Scripture quotations in this volume are from the King James Version of the Bible.

Library of Congress Cataloging in Publication Data

Spillman, James Russell,
  Omega cometh.
    1. End of the world. 2. Man (Christian theology)
3. Church. I. Title.
BT876.S68   230   79-9297
ISBN 0-8007-1071-1

Copyright © 1979 by James R. Spillman
Published by Fleming H. Revell Company
All rights reserved
Printed in the United States of America

TO *my darling wife, Nancy*

She has been a sympathetic critic and encourager, a manuscript typist—really a co-author. The message in *Omega Cometh* is not just mine but hers also.

Contents

Omega Cometh

1

These Are the Last Days! These Are the Last Days!

The Sky Is Falling! The Sky Is Falling!

Chicken Little's exclamation of impending doom echoes down the corridor of years from childhood until now. The fable of the falling sky was meant for the ears of little children. But in recent years adults, too, have heard and feared the warning, and have seen the declaration that "the world is coming to an end" paralleled by the ominous circumstances of real life.

Chicken Little was nothing but an alarmist and clucked her way to an incorrect conclusion. But today there are those more sober and serious who join that foolish hen. They have the uneasy feeling that the state of the sky, and the world that's under it, is shaky, and that the termination of our world as we know it is no children's nursery story.

Today we do not need nursery stories to make us aware that the world is indeed coming to an end. The signs of the times are obvious to all who have eyes to see and ears to hear. The signs are political, ecological, physical, and cultural. They are spiritual, too, and we shall see that they are biblical.

11

The Russians Are Coming! The Russians Are Coming!

During World War I, the Russian Revolution took place. In the years that followed, as the Communist government established its severe and dictatorial policies, it was obvious that this kind of political apparatus was anathema to Western countries. Heretofore, the Russian bear had been difficult to associate with, capricious, uniquely oblique, but at least friendly. But now he was appearing downright warlike—in peacetime yet!

As the war clouds were forming in the 1930s in central Europe, the Russians continued to be surly, standoffish, and secretive. Five-year plans, designed to establish industry and increase production, were put into operation. During this time, the USSR was making tremendous industrial gains. As she was particularly concerned with Japan's proximity, much of the industrial production was military in nature. The bear, in hibernation for so long, was now stretching and strengthening.

In 1940, Hitler attacked Russia with his blitzkrieg hell. Germany's pulverizing panzers advanced dozens of miles every day, scorching the earth and annihilating Russian armies as they went. Not thousands, but millions were killed. Russia reeled; defeat seemed certain. Then two things happened: a very early Russian winter, with temperatures as low as seventy-five degrees below zero, and American aid. The United States sent billions of dollars of land-lease war matériel to Russia. The Hun was stopped. The war was won, and Russia had moved from a giant of geography to a giant in the international body politic.

With the industrial velocity gained through a total-war economy and the unmatched generosity of the United States, Russia now assumed her place as a superpower. The 1950s and 1960s found her erecting iron curtains throughout the world, stockpiling atomic bombs, and rattling missiles in America's direction. In the 1970s, we have witnessed a manifold increase in her nuclear and conventional military power, posing an ominous threat to the favorable balance of power which heretofore has shielded the United States. What will the 1980s bring?

America's responses to Russia during these years have been many and varied. They have ranged from NATO treaties to the Berlin airlift, from backyard bomb shelters to McCarthy witch-hunts, from the cold war to the hot Cuban missile crisis, from cultural exchange to massive wheat deals, from SALT talks to the now famous détente.

Theologians and prophecy teachers have dusted off their eschatological charts to teach once again of Gog and Magog, and the armies of the North. Armageddon seems closer.

Amidst the cries of warning and the hustle and bustle of defense and deterrence stands this fact: The bear is moving methodically westward.

From the Bear to the Dragon

Now let us go from foraging bear to coiled dragon. In all of the history of the world, no nation has loomed as large or as potentially powerful as Communist China. She is the giant of giants. (She is numerically Russia doubled and the United States doubled with Central America thrown in.) In the past several years she has moved from isolation and economic and political obscurity to prominence and power in the family of nations. Her vast manpower resources are incalculable. She is an emerging member of the nuclear family, a family that is growing rapidly.

If China continues on her present course of development, she will in time have sufficient power and influence to challenge the United States naval and air supremacy in the Pacific. The control of Southeast Asia could well fall to her by default.

Can anyone gainsay this? Already China has militarily and politically confronted the West twice and has yet to lose. Albeit the confrontations were by remote-control political extensions called North Korea and Southeast Asia, they were power confrontations, and they were important. In the parlance of competition, the West tied the former and lost the latter!

Culturally, China had for centuries been shredded by divisions of tradition and language. In spite of her classical accomplishments a la Marco Polo, the masses remained illiterate. Since the Communist takeover, the people have been molded into a viable unit. They now read and write one language, Maoist script, a simplified Mandarin. In a large measure, illiteracy has been eliminated. The dragon has been sent to school, and the world is wondering what it is learning and just when it will graduate!

The Supers and the Semisupers

There are three superpowers in the world. They are the United States, Russia, and Communist China. The two semisuperpowers are West Germany and Japan. Even though the economic ties of Japan and West Germany with the United States are enormous and complex, they hardly fall into the category of "longtime friends."

Other countries, of course, exercise very important economic and political influence, such as France, Great Britain, Australia, Italy, and so forth, but they are countries on their way up or on their way down. None has the economic clout of Japan or West Germany. So far, through military and trade agreements financed mostly with American dollars, these two semisupers have held in tight with America. But, let us suppose that the ever-weakening military-assistance lines were snapped by one or more of a number of possible pressures. These could be anything from the gradual corrosion of basic ideological difference to the simultaneous military stance of Russia toward West Germany and of Communist China toward Japan. If the military line frays and snaps, then the always "iffy" financial line would be put to a severe strain, probably to the breaking point.

Today it is easy to see the world polarized into two camps: Communist and non-Communist. If the United States-Japan-West Germany break came, there would be a frantic political scramble that would leave the United States with the proverbial short end of the stick.

The purpose here is not to diagram an end-time coalition for global catastrophe, but simply to attempt to point out one of the many ways a war threshold can be established in these days of "wars and rumours of wars" (Matthew 24:6). Conclusively, it can be said that in this completely untenable international situation, wars and prewar conflicts cannot be averted.

Fights in the School Yard

While the big powers improve new military techniques, smaller countries, like small boys, square off in the international school yard.

Ireland continues its "religio-political" war that has plagued its people for generations.

South Africa's racial conflict escalates daily. Experts predict a bloody war with international repercussions.

Central America seethes and smokes. Honduras and El Salvador fight sporadically, while Guatemala and Belize coldly regard one another.

Cuba is generally bellicose to any democracy, with soldiers serving in Angola and in a number of South American
family squabbles.

Turkey and Greece are in uneasy truce and appear likely
to stay that way.

Israel and Arab allied countries are on a constant war
footing.

The causes of wars seem to be more plentiful now than
ever in man's violent history. John Davidson said it well in
his poem "War Song":

> Some diplomats no doubt
> Will launch a heedless word,
> And lurking war leap out.
>
> And blood in torrents pour
> In vain—always in vain,
> For war breeds war again.

Where Have All the Flowers Gone?

Few thinking persons have not been touched by the cur-
rent ecological world crisis. The depletion of natural resources, the "wearing out" of tillable soil, the natural pollution of man and the unnatural pollution of industry have
caused us to begin programs of conservation and re-
plenishment. The cry that we are losing our naturalness is a
cry of truth. Our wild flowers and our wildlife are disappear-
ing with the world's ever-diminishing wilderness.

Linked to the inability to retain our naturalness is the
inability to adequately feed our people. The world food
supply continues to dwindle in spite of increased efforts
toward more planting and better yield. What is the problem? Will it get worse? If so, how much worse?

The countries and continents historically least able to

feed their masses are in greater trouble now than ever before. China, Russia, India, Central and South America, and Africa are the most vulnerable. The greatest population explosion has been in these areas. Even the great world breadbasket, the United States, is having problems.

No Longer in the Dell

For a country that started in farmers' fields, we certainly have changed! The children's play song that goes, "Hi Ho the merrio, The farmer in the dell," goes on to state that "the farmer takes a wife." It never says where the farmer took his wife, but he must have taken her to Philadelphia, Chicago, Manhattan, or Los Angeles.

When Abraham Lincoln was elected president in 1860, our country was a rural nation. In 1925, we still had more than 50 million farmers—over half the population of the country. Today, official government figures report barely 9 million farmers. Mechanized farm equipment allows each farmer to till more soil; chemical fertilizers have given us better per-acre yields. But chemistry has backfired. It now takes more and more chemical fertilizer, such as anhydrous ammonia, to produce normal yields. The soil actually becomes an ammonia "junky" as it becomes addicted to the petroleum-based plant food. And being petroleum based—with petroleum scarce and its prices soaring out of sight—farmers are not able to use as much as they would like or need.

Everybody Talks About the Weather

A farmer friend of mine said, "We only have two kinds of weather, usual and unusual, and it is usually unusual."

In mid 1976, the Central Intelligence Agency of the United States published a startling and fearful report on world food growth and supply as a result of weather that creates famine conditions. The report predicted armed violence in the wake of food shortages.

This gloomy study took for granted that the world had entered a period of cooler temperatures that will cause substantial decreases in crop yields. It went on to predict that this will result in political and economic unrest and large-scale migration backed by military force. Can we imagine the awful religious war that could be caused by Chinese soldiers moving into India to round up the millions of sacred cows to feed China's hungry?

The CIA report concluded that national attempts would be made to modify the climate, with detrimental effects on neighboring nations, resulting in population losses comparable to those which occurred between 1600 and 1850. (Remember the terrible stories of the great famines?)

Is the weather changing? The answer is yes, and the change is for the worse. The jet stream, a high-speed wind that flows across the United States at high-altitude levels and greatly influences weather, shifted to the north in the winter of 1976, resulting in the diversion of snow from the Great Plains and the Corn Belt states.

The Northern Hemisphere's oceans have cooled significantly in the past decade, decreasing the amount of moisture falling in the Soviet Union.

Sunspot activity is at a low point, and in the past, this has coincided with extreme drought.

All of these changing meteorological conditions spell lack of rain, drought, and low crop yields. Couple this projection with the mid-1976 food reserve report by Jerald Ciekot, of the World Hunger Project of the American Friends Service Committee, in New York City, and there is cause for global fear. Ciekot reported that as recently as 1970, the world had about ninety days of grain supplies in reserve, including the potential of idled American cropland. At the time of his report, United States farmland was in full use and grain reserves were down to a frightening thirty-day supply! Ciekot's conclusion was: "We are now living a hand-to-mouth existence." (If that was the case in mid 1976, how much worse it must be now.)

Old Mother Hubbard's Cupboard

Population increases, pollution, urban shift, fertilizer backlash, and changing climates have joined to threaten famine in our immediate future. Not that we are totally unaware of this scourge. History recalls "spot" or area famines in the 1800s. We have come to expect periodic famines in the densely populated arid countries of Africa and India. But these "local" famines cannot be compared to the horrendous foodlessness that now threatens our world. We are now over four billion in number and millions more join the food line every month.

Old Mother Hubbard can no longer be taken as a quaint nursery rhyme. Her bare cupboard reflects stark reality.

The Other Ugly Sister

Famine's ugly sister is malnutrition and disease. When the body is robbed of necessary nutriments for daily functioning, malnutrition sets in. Disease follows almost automatically. Normal sanitation precautions are carelessly abused and forgotten. Drinking water becomes premium. Nature's balance of who eats whom and what is critically upset. The animal kingdom makes food forays into the human kingdom. When all of these situations join forces against man, there is one result: pestilence. Pestilence is one disease that has become widespread and deadly. The results of famine as predicted are global in scope. The associated diseases share that same global dimension.

A Whole Lot of Shaking Going On

A dear friend of mine who lives in California recently exclaimed: "I've never heard as much about earthquakes in my whole life as I have heard this past year!" My friend is right. Never was more written or more spoken about earthquakes than in the last decade. Guatemala's crippling quake in the spring of 1976, killing thirty thousand and leaving one million homeless, is a notable example.

The earthquake center in Pasadena, California, reports that there are earthquakes of varying Richter Scale magnitudes every single day. The earth is literally shaking itself into a frenzy.

Earthquake monitoring has for years been a meticulous scientific discipline, but now scientists of the world can often accurately predict their occurrence and magnitude. Earthquake "presence" has become so commonplace that in southern California the people live with a constant concern for the "big one."

Doctor Stephen Plagemann and Dr. John R. Gribbin, authors of *The Jupiter Effect,* have even gone so far as to predict that Los Angeles will be destroyed in the spring of 1982 by a massive earthquake triggered by the super conjunction of all nine planets which will occur at that time. This is difficult to dismiss since both authors have impeccable scientific credentials.

The Culture Revolution

In four short decades our country has gone through its most serious revolution, from Christian to non-Christian, from a God-centered base to a man-centered base. It is true, of course, that not everyone in the 1930s was Christian, as it is true that not everyone in the 1970s was non-Christian. However, in this short span, we have changed from a Christian consensus to the disappearance of that consensus. Christianity in America, in cultural emphasis and cultural result, is in the minority. If, in the 1930s, you had asked people at random in Central Park, New York City, a question on the true nature of Christianity, you probably would have received positive, informed replies. Perhaps they all would not have been born-again Christians, but they would have understood the rudiments of the basic Christian message. If you attempted to ask the same question today (assuming you wouldn't be mugged or murdered as a result of your inquiry), you would find that few have a concept of true Christianity. They are not just ignorant of the biblical facts of personal salvation; it is more than this. The whole culture has shifted from Christian to non-Christian.

It is a catastrophe of major proportions to see our Christian culture disappear in the quicksand of apathy and unbelief in a mere forty years.

I find it significant that, in the forty years it has taken our country to move from rural to urban, from 50 million farmers to 9 million farmers, our Christian culture has become morally barren. I must agree with Francis Schaeffer, there is "death in the city." We have congregated, crowded, consumed, constructed, and now we are convulsing in the coagulation of our own moral clot!

Triumph of "Ungood" and "Unlove"

As superindustrialization has been assaulting our American culture and personal character, two other amoral enemies have been attacking our exposed flanks. The army of relativism (all things are relative; nothing is absolute) overwhelmed our left, while the army of secularism (nothing is holy) converged upon our right. While industry was pushing us up the technological ladder toward things and more things, we found ourselves treed by the triumphant "relative" and "secular." Doctor Ungood and Dr. Unlove now surround us.

To be "cool" (a four-letter word meaning tough, unsquare, and unworried) is the "in" attitude. It is not cool to respect established mores. Doctor Benjamin Spock and the school of permissive child psychology came in. His teachings were "right on" to this "hang-loose" generation. As the nuclear family and the home ran into trouble, each institution of authority in turn was affected: law enforcement, civilian government, and finally the armed forces.

Individuals are encouraged to "do their own thing." The moral authority of the church is smiled at. People stay away from the church in ever-increasing numbers. After an enormous postwar boom, denominational religion peaked out and began a decline that continues yearly.

Marriage, once the citadel of Christendom, balances upon an ever-shakier foundation. Unlove paved the way for hatred, while Ungood was propagandizing betrayal and deception. The roving eye encouraged the roving hand, and the hand pulled the curtain of duplicity around illicit sexual affairs. No marriage can take much of this kind of malaffection. From instability to alienation is one step, and from alienation to divorce is just one more. Americans were divorced and continue to be divorced in horrifying numbers.

The children are the big losers. They should have been taught absolutes at home, but instead they have learned relatives at school. They should have learned spiritual lessons at home and church, but rather they have learned secular lessons at school and in the street. They should have learned the Christian view of sex at home, but they have had to learn the clinical view at school and the corrupt view in the neighborhood alley.

When the foundations of our homes and families began to erode, the foundation of our country began to slide. Ungood and Unlove have triumphed, but thank God it is only a tentative triumph.

America Looks Eastward and Inward

The culture revolution pretty well disintegrated our national Christian base. When the foundation for absolute love and absolute good is gone, men are left to their own designs and fantasies, or they seek the exotica of expanded experiences.

Prophets, gurus, and self-proclaimed messiahs from the East made their way to our shores. While denominational churches were losing followers, men such as Mahareshi Yogi were gaining converts. Americans, disillusioned and dissatisfied, learned how to assume the "lotus position" and alter their state of consciousness.

Some who didn't want to follow Yogi's brand of yoga decided to follow the adolescent Maharaj Ji, of the Divine Light Mission, who claimed to be the Perfect Master! Both of these sects now claim hundreds of thousands of adherents in the United States.

In the last twenty years, we have seen literally dozens of new gurus and expanded-consciousness prophets setting up shop and leading the naive astray. Has anyone not seen the shaven heads of the Hare Krishnas and heard their mesmeric chanting? Hardly an airport or public place has not been invaded by these book-selling chanters in their saffron robes.

One of the more popular men of the East is the Reverend Sun Moon of Korea. He bills himself as the messiah that has been promised in the Bible. His Unification Church almost exclusively zeroes in on young people. They are evangelized, then taken to indoctrination camps where they are brainwashed and programmed with his strange moralistic apostasy. Once programmed, young "Moonies" take to the streets to sell flowers in a money-raising hustle that would make Elmer Gantry wince.

Many other cults have arrived from the East, too numerous to discuss here; they have joined a parade of prophets seeking the minds and hearts of the young.

Besides the totally brainwashed, there are some who think that part of what the Eastern magi have to say is acceptable, but stop short of buying the whole package. This has resulted in Western mutations of Eastern religions. Some have developed a Western-style yoga—more physical and mental than cultural. Transcendental Meditation caught on big. The Americanized version is called T.M., which has made tremendous inroads into the typical American scene: businesses, schools, clubs, churches, and lodges.

One of the fastest-growing awareness groups is *est. Est* was formed by Werner Erhard, an American of German extraction who abandoned his wife and four children, failed as a salesman of success-motivation material, and leapt into the new self-awareness business. Erhard charms his followers by stating that *est* is nothing and that real life is nothing. Problems are nothing. In fact, everything is nothing. In the neonihilism of *est* you get nothing for something (about $250 for the initial encounter).

Many other awareness groups are fishing for pilgrims— ranging from Biofeedback to Science of the Mind, from Timothy Leary's LSD to Rev. Ike's "You can't lose with the stuff I use."

Alvin Toffler, author of *Future Shock,* said it well when he said, "America has all the symptoms of a man having a nervous breakdown." This nervous breakdown is the result of our spiritual breakdown. It is long past time that this nation stopped looking eastward for the mysterious wisdom of the ancients, stopped looking inward for expanded self-awareness, and began looking upward, for "our redemption draweth nigh" (*see* Luke 21:28).

The Last Word on the Last Days

Dozens of Scriptures in the Old and the New Testaments speak of "final" or "end" or "last" days. The major and the minor prophets speak to this. The Book of Revelation is not only the last book in the Bible but it is also an end-time book.

As Christians living in this wonderful era of grace, we are particularly interested in the end of days as we know them and the return of our Lord Jesus Christ. There is, perhaps, no account of the "last days" in Scripture more complete or more clear than the discourse Jesus gave His disciples after one of His temple visits. This discourse is found in three of the four Gospels. The references are Matthew 24:3–51; Mark 13:4–37; and Luke 21:7–36.

As the Matthew reference is somewhat more complete, let us look at a portion of it:

> And as he sat upon the mount of Olives, the disciples came unto him privately, saying, Tell us, when shall these things be? and what shall be the sign of thy coming, and of the end of the world? And Jesus answered and said unto them, Take heed that no man deceive you. For many shall come in my name, saying, I am Christ; and shall deceive many. And ye shall hear of wars and rumours of wars: see that ye be not troubled: for all these things must come to pass, but the end is not yet. For nation shall rise against nation, and kingdom against kingdom: and there

shall be famines, and pestilences, and earthquakes, in divers places. All these are the beginning of sorrows. Then shall they deliver you up to be afflicted, and shall kill you: and ye shall be hated of all nations for my name's sake. And then shall many be offended, and shall betray one another, and shall hate one another. And many false prophets shall rise, and shall deceive many. And because iniquity shall abound, the love of many shall wax cold. But he that shall endure unto the end, the same shall be saved. And this gospel of the kingdom shall be preached in all the world for a witness unto all nations; and then shall the end come.

Matthew 24:3–14

In verse 3, the disciples ask three questions: (1) When shall these things be? (2) What shall be the sign of Jesus' coming? (3) What is the sign for the end of the world?

Jesus doesn't answer any of these questions immediately, but rather warns of men who would seek to deceive, presumably concerning the things about which the disciples had just asked, that is, dates and signs. He goes on to say that many shall come and attempt to deceive, and many will be deceived. Apparently Christ is warning the disciples against sign givers and date setters. The day and hour of His coming are positively to be kept a secret: "But of that day and hour knoweth no man . . ." (Matthew 24:36). However, the three questions can still be answered, as they do not specifically ask for the day and hour.

These particular Scriptures, especially Matthew 24:6–14, are a perfect fit for our days. Let us deal with the signs as Scripture presents them.

"Wars and rumours of wars" and "nation shall rise against nation"—there is such total awareness today of these prophecies that we may honestly conclude that there is universal agreement on this perilous condition.

"And kingdom against kingdom"—this, in part, refers to

the preceding, but not entirely. This quotation means the embattlement of spiritual kingdoms, too. (Ephesians 6:10–18 teaches of our war against spiritual adversaries.) And we are witnesses of the constant battle of subkingdoms against other subkingdoms, such as labor versus management, liberal versus conservative, father versus son. In these days, kingdoms seem to have built-in conflict and antipathy to other kingdoms.

"And there shall be famines"—we can only add that hardly a newspaper can be picked up today that does not report a food shortage or a new famine somewhere in the world.

"And pestilences"—disease, in large and deadly doses, always follows famine.

"And earthquakes, in divers places"—the California Institute of Technology's equipment irrefutably proves that earthquakes occur daily in the world, and they are "in divers places."

"Then shall they deliver you up to be afflicted, and shall kill you: and ye shall be hated of all nations . . ."—this kind of persecution is nineteen hundred years old, but it continues today, especially in Communist countries. Many expect it to become far worse and spread even farther around the globe.

"And then shall many be offended, and shall betray one another, and shall hate one another"—we see betrayal and hate around us now, and as times worsen, so will these cruel attitudes.

"And many false prophets shall rise, and shall deceive many"—false prophets are so numerous today that we can even find them listed in the Yellow Pages.

"And because iniquity shall abound, the love of many shall wax cold"—again, read the daily paper!

Now the zinger for the zealous:

"And this gospel of the kingdom shall be preached in all the world for a witness unto all nations; and then shall the end come."

Isn't that tremendous? These signs of the times are manifest *before* the entire world has been presented with the Gospel. "All the world" is yet to hear of Jesus Christ! These signs of the times tell us that these are the last days, but before the end comes, the Gospel will be preached to all men everywhere. What a promise! What a joy! What a task!

How is it possible? In nineteen hundred years we have fallen behind. We are further behind now than one hundred years ago, when just one billion people were in the world. We now have over four billion people on earth. How can we ever reach them? The Census Bureau predicts that we will hit five billion in just a few more years. The task seems impossible. It is numerical nonsense to think it can be done. But God has promised. He always keeps His promises, and He has a special strategy for this seemingly impossible task. We must continue trusting that He controls the times and tides of men.

Robert Browning wrote:

> The best is yet to be,
> The last of life, for which the first was made.
> Our times are in his hand.

2

Omega Times

For in the fatness of these pursy times
Virtue itself of vice must pardon beg.
WILLIAM SHAKESPEARE

Alpha and Omega

Revelation 21:6 states, "I am Alpha and Omega, the beginning and the end. I will give unto him that is athirst of the fountain of the water of life freely."

Alpha and *omega* are the first and last letters of the Greek alphabet. In the above passage, our Lord tells us that as the *Alpha,* He was and is the Creator, or beginner of all things. This truth is stated succinctly in John 1:3: "All things were made by him; and without him was not any thing made that was made."

He goes on to speak of Himself as the *Omega.* That is, He is the starter and the finisher, the beginner and the ender. Hebrews' writer explained the same relationship as ". . . Jesus the author and finisher of our faith" (Hebrews 12:2).

Not only is He the perfecter of what He began in initial creation, but as He inhabited the first, or creation days, He also inhabits these last, or completion days. God, of course,

29

always finishes or perfects whatever He begins (*see* Philippians 1:6; 2 Samuel 22:31; Hebrews 12:2).

God did not create man in a creation caprice to see how he would turn out. Man was not a Pavlovian experiment conducted in the laboratory of the Eden paradise. God did not arrange all the good trees in an orchard maze around the bad tree to see if the man-rat would disobey the order of the day. Rather, man was made in the image of God that in all things he might glorify and honor God. Scripture allows us to believe that this was God's original or *alpha* purpose. Apparently God's original plan was thwarted by man's rebellious disobedience, but His *alpha* purpose has remained intact and in process.

Man's rebellion broke the original relationship between God and man, but Christ's redemption bought and brought it back again. Regardless of the change in plan, God's purpose never changed. His purposes are inextricably interrelated to His character, and His character never changes (*see* Hebrews 13:8).

Conclusively, God's purpose for man, having begun in creation or *alpha* days, is now being completed in these last, or *omega* days. These are "finishing" days, "perfecting" days, "completing" days. These are *omega* days!

Days That Never Were and Scarcely Are!

We have discussed the "signs of the times," the dangers of the present day. We have put them into the category of "last days," and paralleled them to scriptural "last days" passages.

Now let us talk about today. The average urbanite wakes up daily to far more stimuli than he can respond to. He lives in a haze of "overchoice." He is bombarded with ten times more sensory stimuli than his father ever was—a hundred times more than his grandfather. Our average urbanite is a terrified tightwire walker. He tries to ease his way along the thin wire of meaning stretched loosely over a chasm of nothingness. Those who watch yell words of advice and criticism—much criticism. He is at the same time angry and afraid, frustrated and tired, depressed yet hopeful. What can he do? He cannot go back, though many have tried. He cannot stop. There is horror in the thought of falling. He must go on, but to what? Where? Why? How did our man get so hooked and hung up? Life wasn't always this way. What happened?

The 800th Lifetime

Alvin Toffler calls this accelerated life-style we are experiencing today, the 800th lifetime. His reasoning goes something like this:

    (1) Man is circa fifty thousand years old.
    (2) His average life span is sixty-two years.
    (3) This totals about eight hundred lifetimes.

Allowing Toffler the assumption that we did begin 50,000 years ago, let us quote more. The first 650 lifetimes, according to Toffler, would have to have been spent in caves. Only during the last 70 lifetimes has man been able to communicate effectively from one lifetime to the other. Only in the last 6 lifetimes has man been able to see the printed word. Only in the last 4 lifetimes have we been able to measure time with any precision. Only the last 2 have seen the use of the electric motor. The overwhelming majority of material goods we use now originated in this, our 800th lifetime.

This is rather impressive acceleration and development. *Change*. That is the key word. Life for us has changed so rapidly and so completely that we have had to try to "unlearn" faster than we once learned.

For thousands of years we milked "Old Bossy," the family cow, by hand. In this lifetime the automatic milking machine has kept our hands clean, and it is more efficient in every way. But before we had the chance to enjoy the new labor-saving device, we moved to the city and left Old Bossy in the hands of a multimillion-dollar dairy conglomerate. We not only have lost that fond family friend but we have also forgotten how to milk by hand.

Our entire life-style, particularly as it relates to our primary survival agreement with the land, repeats the story. Our disavowal of the rural and subsequent enchantment with the urban have not just incidentally changed our circumstances, they have essentially changed our character.

Within a single lifetime, agriculture, the historic basis for civilization, has lost its dominance. Fifty years ago over half of America lived on the farm. Now less than five percent live on the farm, and the number is still shrinking.

If agriculture is the first stage of economic development and industrialism is the second, we can now be said to be in the third stage, the "service economy." In the mid 1940s, the United States became the first nation of prominence in which more than half of the nonfarm labor force traded in their factory blue collars for white ones.

For the first time in history, one civilization, in one lifetime, threw off the yoke of agriculture and the yoke of manual labor as well. No wonder we think things are changing so fast; they are!

I was born in 1934. Today the world is as different from the time in which I was born as that world was different from Alexander the Great's. I was born in the middle of human history. More has happened since then than in all the thousands of years before. No wonder man has trouble coping. Toffler concludes concisely, "Change is avalanching upon our heads, and most people are grotesquely unprepared to cope with it."

No Deposit—No Return

Our society has an impermanent core. Because of the accelerated changes now attacking us with machine-gun rapidity, we have ceased to live or even to think in the realm of permanence.

Our economy, once based on the permanence of agriculture and the land, is now based on commodities and production. We have moved from an economy of permanence to an economy of transience. Superindustrialization has ordained it. Our technology and production methods, all machine centered, have made it cheaper to acquire the new rather than to repair the old. Soft-drink bottles are a prime example. A new bottle can be made for less than it takes to collect, clean, and refill the old one.

Advancing technology allows us to improve the product as time goes by. To be locked into an unchangeable, permanent product would stifle the technology of improvement, stifle competition, and turn products into relics in short order. Recognizing the changing needs in our changing society, we are hesitant to commit our product to any long-range technology and its attendant expense.

This doctrine of disposability has made us into a throw-away society. Easy come, easy go. Our disposable diapers, food containers, handkerchiefs, razors, hair curlers, and such, have paved the way for disposable paper pajamas, bed sheets, and even wedding gowns.

One of the sad side effects of this no-deposit, no-return society is that it teaches us to dispose of unwanted or unnecessary items. This carries over into people-to-people relationships and people-to-God relationships. If someone does something that is uncomfortable or unwanted, then we feel justified about using the doctrine of disposability and simply throw away the relationship.

This is especially true of the jeans generation, young people who have been taught to semicommit in a casual, open-minded manner. They have been weaned on the watery milk of transience and impermanence, and for the most part, their personal relationships do not last as long as their jeans.

Disposability also characterizes our man-God relationships. If there is a Bible truth that is uncomfortable or that makes us feel uneasy, we simply dispose of it—usually by ignoring it—and dwell upon the more palatable promises. A good example is the subject of hell. How long has it been since you've heard a forthright sermon on hell?

Rent-a-Thing

If we are unable to buy it and dispose of it, we most assuredly can rent it. Everything that can be owned can be rented. If it is your desire to spend the summer in New York, you simply rent a seat on a plane to get there, rent an apartment when you get there, and rent a car to see where you've gotten!

Minimum involvement is what the user of disposable containers gets for his money. In a sense he purchases noninvolvement. The same goes for the renter. Renting a home carries considerably less responsibility and involvement than purchasing a home. (Homes are too expensive to throw away.) Renting implies short-term commitment, and in our transient, changing society long-term commitment is shunned like the plague.

Noncommitment or short-term-commitment practice cannot help but foster the same response in the realm of spiritual relationships. Christendom is saturated with church and meeting hoppers. They don't buy into any situation or church by joining the membership and helping shoulder the responsibilities. Rather, they read the newspaper to see who is speaking where and follow the glitter from place to place. In a sense they are engaging in "rent a blessing" or even "rent a church."

Just a note here to the prudent: Jesus didn't "rent" our salvation. He purchased it fully and completely. It is total responsibility and is definitely long-term.

Jet-Age Gypsies

Twenty-five years ago a man wanted to buy a house and settle down. Now, the same man wants to rent a camper and run around. Acquaintances of mine in Los Angeles daily commute by air to work in San Francisco. For three years, a Denver minister flew to Los Angeles weekly to spend two days taping a radio program, then flew back to Denver to hold church services each Sunday.

I have gone by air to speak in three different churches in three different cities, all in the same day. It is common for a Los Angeles dweller to commute via freeway seventy-five miles to work and back every day.

We are a moving generation. Distances do not frighten us as they did our grandfathers. Never in history has distance meant less. Man's relationship with place has never been so fragile, so temporary. Place used to mean security, both emotional and financial. It carried with it the value of lasting personal relationships. It meant memories of good times, and not-so-bad times. Most of all, it meant home, the center of interpersonal values, and love—much love.

Now place means none of these things save in a most transitory way. Figuratively, we use up places much as we use up soft-drink containers, with much the same result: no deposit, no return. We are witnessing a decline in the significance of place to mankind.

Each year over forty million Americans, not counting children under one year, move their residences. This figure comprises more than the total population of Cambodia, Ghana, Guatemala, Honduras, Israel, Mongolia, Nicaragua, and Tunisia combined. It is as if the total population of all these countries had suddenly been relocated.

This kind of nomadism causes us to be physically and emotionally disoriented and confused. It tends to make us fickle and careless in our responsibilities, especially in the realm of finances. It pushes us into cowardice. We tend to run, to escape a pressure or unsavory situation. Finally, it gives us a false sense of security by allowing us to think that we can outmaneuver or outrun any problem.

In contrast, it is interesting to note that Jesus lived thirty of His thirty-three years in one little town. Even after He began ministering, He never traveled more than one hundred miles from the place of His youth. The whole concept and experience of mobility has changed drastically from foot power and horsepower to electric power and jet power. Our world has become larger in every way except in the areas of communication and transportation.

It is easy for us to see how this accelerative thrust in society affects the individual. The parallel of shrinking place and shriveling relationships is all too evident. Transiency, availability, and mobility have pressed us toward what Martin Buber calls an "I-it" relationship. This "I-it," which in reality is an "unrelationship," must be transformed to the "I-thou" relationship. The former smacks of selfishness. The latter forecasts fulfillment.

Temporary Man

Great mobility and disposability have spawned a sense of freedom without responsibility. We are able to meet and greet a lot of people in a short period of time. We go to conventions, or go on vacation, and hundreds of new people flow into our river of relationship. This momentary relationship can be intense and very personal, but as the people of that place are exchanged for the people of the next place, the names fade and the faces become fuzzy. As these experiences multiply, we feel less and less responsibility toward other people and their situations.

After a while, a great temporariness envelops us. It is this temporariness that we see accelerating at the same rate that our superindustrialization accelerates. Toffler said it best: "For just as things and places flow through our lives at a faster clip, so, too, do people."

Because of this, we must pay a high price if we seek to establish a deeper or more lasting involvement. If one is a city dweller (and the great majority of Americans are), clearly close ties with all acquaintances are impossible. In fact, to try to maintain such ties would turn one into a psychiatrist's nightmare.

Today, too, we meet each other in specific roles. The time and involvement we give to the mailman, the store clerk, and the taxicab driver are different from what we would give to our fellow worker. The time and involvement we give to our fellow worker is less than what we give to a close family member.

The more people we meet, the more organizationally involved we are, the greater our desire for deeper relationships, the more complex the whole matter becomes. Usually this leads us to define our relationships with the people we meet in functional terms. "If he is a good mechanic, he can work on my car regardless of his social incompetence or religious preferences." "If he is a competent dentist, I will let him drill on my teeth even though I know nothing of his personal life."

We have created the disposable person. We now have Toffler's "Modular Man." In reality, we do not relate to the whole person, but simply plug into a "module" of his total personality. In this, we find a relationship that we consider safe and functional.

Before we decry this way of life as wholly paganistic and insensitive, let us consider it further. This is part of what Francis Schaeffer meant when he said there is "death in the city." Harvey Cox, eminent theologian and author of *The Secular City,* affirms that emotional emptiness and self-destruction await the one attempting to be involved with everyone. The problem, of course, is that every relationship involves mutual demands and expectations. The tighter a relationship, the greater the demands. The more involved the relationship, the higher the expectations.

The closer the friend, the greater the hurt. Every time a family moves, it tends to slough off friends—even close friends. No matter how we try to maintain contact, we usually fail. Invariably, new friends take the place of old—at least in function, if not in fondness. We have become members of a social literati. We turn in old friends for new like books in a library.

We have observed that most married couples tend to list between seven and twelve as the number of close friends they have. The men list less, the women more. Men seem to be able to exchange an old friend for a new quicker and easier than women.

This accelerated rate of transience, mobility, and technology has molded the American city dweller into a "person warp" of ugly proportions. The "urbanoxia" of our society is now being inhaled by the "Temporary Man."

This Modular, or Temporary Man, is caught in a maelstrom of forces that are beyond his ken. He spins in a whirlpool of change.

(1) His world is out of control in respect to conflict—"wars and rumours of wars."

(2) National and international boundaries have become vulnerable—"Nation shall rise against nation."

(3) Every organization or life group is in conflict with at least one other—"and kingdom against kingdom."

(4) There is not enough food to feed the earth's four billion inhabitants, and projected crop losses and weather conditions declare that the future will be worse than the present—"and there shall be famines."

(5) New diseases have been added to deadly old ones. Medical costs are too high to pay. Malpractice insurance rates are driving doctors out of practice. There are more sick people in the world now than there were people in the world in 1875—"and pestilences."

(6) Earthquakes and associated natural disasters are frequent—"and earthquakes, in divers places."

(7) People do not have the love and dedication they had for each other in years gone by—"Then shall many be offended, and shall betray one another, and shall hate one another."

(8) Religion is so confusing! He does not know whom to believe—"And many false prophets shall rise, and shall deceive many."

(9) He is afraid to walk the streets at night—"Iniquity shall abound."

(10) Everything is changing so fast that he cannot keep up.

(11) He seeks permanence in an impermanent society.

(12) He himself feels that he is nonessential, disposable.

(13) He has personal needs in an impersonal society.

(14) He is so mobile that he moves too much.

(15) Old values are questioned; new values are difficult to evaluate.

(16) He is forced to depend upon more and more people, but they become less and less dependable.

(17) The world economic system is a bust, his financial situation precarious.

(18) Education did not give him the utopia that it promised. He sees janitors with Ph.D. degrees and he sees space scientists pumping gasoline at the corner station.

(19) He doesn't trust politics or politicians—and they are the ones who try to run this confusion.

(20) He has been used, abused, and discarded by those he called dear friends.

What can the Temporary Man do with this unhappy drama in which he stars every day? He has valiantly tried to make the old life work, to no avail. He has tried every endeavor within his power, only to fail. What must he do to be saved?

First, he must realize that this old life won't work and that he needs a new life in Jesus Christ. He needs to live in the new dimension—the spirit dimension. He must receive Jesus Christ as Lord and Saviour of his life. He then needs to be filled with the Holy Spirit. Only then can he drop the identity of Temporary Man and become an Eternal Man— God's Omega Man!

3

The Omega Man

The Miracle of the Last Lifetime

The Omega Man: God's prepared instrument for the miracle of the last lifetime. God has prepared a man (*man* is used here strictly as a symbol of men and women) as an instrument of His miraculous grace and power to perfect His latter-day purpose.

Let us again emphasize this purpose. Remember, God has ordained that man should glorify Him. We see this accomplished by man's response to God's redemptive process. God's initial purpose, then, becomes dependent upon a redeemed world (or at least a responsive portion). This purpose has become dynamic in the hearts and lives of regenerated men and women. Christians have been ordered to go "into all the world, and preach the gospel to every creature" (Mark 16:15).

These marching orders, coupled with the promise that before the end of the world, "This gospel of the kingdom shall be preached in all the world for a witness unto all nations . . ." (Matthew 24:14), speak clearly to us. Preaching the Gospel "to every creature" has not been

41

accomplished. It has not been semi-accomplished. He promises us that this will be done before the end comes. If we read the signs of the times correctly, and they are hard to misread, then these are the last days. (It would be easier for us to imagine if we translate "last days" into "last lifetime.")

Urgency and confidence is the unique mixture in this promise of God. To reach the world in one lifetime is patently impossible. How could the church accomplish a work in one lifetime that it has failed to do in fifteen previous lifetimes? It seems to be mathematical malpractice to even consider the possibility!

It took from Creation Day to 1850 (multiplied thousands of years) for the world's population to reach one billion. Two billion population was reached in 1930, just eighty years later. In 1961, a mere thirty-one years later, three billion were counted. In 1976 the world's population reached four billion—a growth of one billion in fifteen years! The immensity of the task to be finished in this last lifetime makes the order to reach every creature seem an impossible one. Can it really be done? What is different in this lifetime from the previous fifteen lifetimes of the church age? Certainly God has not changed (*see* Matthew 28:20). What has changed? What is different?

The answers are simple and powerful. First, God is pouring out His Spirit in unprecedented measure upon the world (*see* Joel 2:28, 29). Second, God has prepared an instrument of ministry unparalleled in church history—the Omega Man!

Who Is He?

The Omega Man is a born-again, Spirit-filled person. He is a product of the superindustrial technosociety, with all of its educational, cultural, and vocational advantages. He is a reservoir of God's last-day Spirit outpouring. he is a part of the finishing of what our heavenly Author started in Eden's paradise.

> The Alpha Adam from his garden cast,
>   to Mount of Law and Mount of Grace.
> His oath will be fulfilled at last
>   by Omega Man, the conclusion race.

Omega Man: A Trichotomy

His Spirit. Recognizing that man is three-in-one—spirit, mind, and body—let us look first at his spirit.

The Apostle Paul refers to this part of man as "the inward man." In 2 Corinthians 4:16, he declares, ". . . yet the inward man is renewed day by day." In chapter 2 he voices his disappointment about not seeing Titus: "I had no rest in my spirit, because I found not Titus my brother" (verse 13).

The Apostle Peter titled the spirit of man as "the hidden man of the heart" (1 Peter 3:4). Peter knew better than any man alive the difference between a spirit that was weak because of the flesh and one that was filled with the power of God.

In fact, man as a spirit was not a subject of common knowledge or understandcng in pre-Pentecostal Bible days. Jesus' confrontation with the Pharisee Nicodemus shows this. Jesus told his night visitor that he must be born again. Nicodemus, with all his religious education and experience, was completely baffled by this statement. He inquired, "How can a man be born when he is old? can he enter the second time into his mother's womb, and be born?" (John 3:4).

Jesus, immediately discerning Nicodemus' deep consternation, explained in childlike, simple terms: "Verily, verily,

I say unto thee, Except a man be born of water and of the Spirit, he cannot enter into the kingdom of God'' (John 3:5). Here we see that water is the agency of physical birth, but the Spirit is the agency of the second birth. Jesus further reinforces this with, "That which is born of the flesh is flesh; and that which is born of the Spirit is spirit" (John 3:6).

When a person is born again, it is his spirit that is born. The new birth is a spiritual renewal. The spirit of man, his only eternal part, passes from eternal death (separation from God) into eternal life. Upon the reception of this new spiritual life, a new responsibility is given. The new one is entrusted to proclaim this Good News to everyone he meets. Spiritual battles, heretofore unimagined, are waged with demonic intensity. The Christian finds that he is not wrestling ". . . against flesh and blood, but against principalities, against powers, against the rulers of the darkness of this world, against spiritual wickedness in high places" (Ephesians 6:12). For this new experience of total spiritual warfare, he finds that he needs total spiritual power.

The Baptism of the Holy Spirit introduces power into the Christian's life. All four Gospels promise this baptism (*see* Matthew 3:11; Mark 1:8; Luke 3:16; and John 1:33). The first chapter of Acts reinforces these four evangel proclamations: ". . . ye shall be baptized with the Holy Ghost . . ." (Acts 1:5) is followed closely by "Ye shall receive power, after that the Holy Ghost is come upon you" (Acts 1:8). The last part of Acts 1:8 declares that those who receive this new power will be witnesses unto God, even "unto the uttermost part of the earth."

There are some today who do not believe that the Baptism of the Holy Spirit is a contemporary experience. They call it a first-century experience, for first-century people, for first-century evangelism. They also assert that the end of the first century saw the end of the Baptism of the Holy Spirit.

Since the character of God and the Word of God are unchangeable (*see* Hebrews 13:8), and His gifts irrevocable (*see* Romans 11:29), such conclusions are untenable. We see today that we have the same message for the same world, from the same God, under the authority of the same commission to stand against the same enemy for the same purpose. It appears unreasonable, unimaginable, and unbiblical not to expect or experience the same baptism.

Another area of misunderstanding in the realm of the Spirit is the fruit-gift controversy. This disagreement has been centered on the listing of the gifts of the Spirit in 1 Corinthians 12:7–11, and the enumeration of the fruit of the Spirit in Galatians 5:22, 23. Although there are other Scriptures involved in this divisionary debate, these two passages are usually situated at ground zero.

The acceptance and manifestation of the fruit of the Spirit are heartily endorsed by both camps. (Who can find grievance with love, joy, and peace?) It is with the acceptance and manifestation of the gifts of the Spirit that the line of demarcation is drawn. There seems to be a diversity of opposition by those who favor fruit over gifts. Tongues, interpretation of tongues, miracles, and healing are solidly opposed, as are discernment of spirits and prophecy. Strangely, faith, wisdom, and knowledge receive only token opposition.

However, as an apologetic of the fruit or gift position is not our purpose, let us proceed.

The Omega Man is involved in the circumstance but not the controversy. His life is to be a ministry of fruit bearing and sharing, and gift receiving and using. His position on gifts of the Spirit must be to receive whatever God gives, and to use what he receives.

His Mind. How to differentiate between the spirit of man and the mind of man? Studies already fill thousands of volumes that are gathering the dust of unuse on the shelves of the ever-learning. Consequently, it would serve no purpose to add to either the volumes or the dust. However, a starting line must be drawn so that the reader can see where the author is "coming from."

The greatest confusion seems centered around the use of the word *soul.* It has been employed as a catchall word that could mean "life," "feelings," "emotions," "personal awareness," or even a combination of "spirit," "mind," and "body." I am not trying to run around a problem here, but the word *soul* and its Greek counterpart *psyche* deserve study. However, since each one is more affinitive than definitive, it would not help us in our goal of making things as simple as possible.

In the final analysis, it is only God who can make the perfect discernment between the spirit and the mind. It is enough for us to understand that the Bible treats the spirit and the mind as separate and distinct entities.

Although this spirit is the only eternal part of man, it harbors alienation and death; it must be reborn. This is the rebirth found in John, chapter 3. The other two parts of man must be renewed. The body will be renewed when this old body (mortal) shall be changed into a new body (immortal) (*see* 1 Corinthians 15:42–57). The mind is to be renewed after the rebirth of the spirit, and before the new body is given (*see* Romans 12:2; Ephesians 4:23).

Knowledge, Knowledge Everywhere and Yet No Time to Think. Today in America information is available on every discipline from the beginning of human history. Everything of general importance that has transpired in the last three thousand years has been recorded. Books have been the main records. But, with the knowledge explosion of the last fifty years, books have not been big enough to absorb the tidal wave of information.

Industrialism created new fields of knowledge and interest that multiplied both in dimension and number the already existing areas of knowledge. Between 1920 and 1950, the world's knowledge reservoir quadrupled.

If the industrial age multiplied the knowledge of the long-standing agricultural age, then superindustrialism has exponentially exploded it. It now takes not only books but also cards, tapes, discs, and films to record the flood of knowledge. Computers have swallowed entire libraries, and with total electronic recall can, on command, regurgitate Einstein, Shakespeare, and Dr. Seuss. Anyone who has done graduate work in a university library remembers well the red eyes from studying microfilm and microfiche. Miniaturization is necessary to store the massive information made available by the explosion of the last few decades.

In all of this, man finds himself daily under verbal assault. Libraries have become storage dumps of nouns and verbs. Computers gorged with ideas, recipes, facts, and theories stand by with an electronic impatience to support coordinated assaults with written, verbal, and visual information.

It is all too much, too fast! It is a blitz of books, an inundation of information. Man has become a victim of alphabet overkill. With his word-wounded mind, man finds it impossible to cope with this pandemic verbfestation. His mind is normal. The situation is not.

A Blue Mood for a Brown Study. Natural man has a normal mind. Since the Fall, man has been unable to employ the full use of his mind. It seems silly to make this kind of statement after stating our unprecedented attainment of knowledge. However, we must see that natural man is where he is because of a multiplying combination of time, people, and machinery. He has grown informationally, but not intellectually. His knowledge is broader, but not deeper. The IQ of today's natural man approximates that of natural man a hundred or a thousand years ago.

The difference is not in natural man's normal mind but rather in the present supernormal situation. While man adhered to the functional simplicity of an agricultural economy and life-style, he coped rather well. While he abided by the rules of the "curse" (". . . cursed is the ground for thy sake; in sorrow shalt thou eat of it all the days of thy life . . . . In the sweat of thy face shalt thou eat bread, till thou return unto the ground . . . ." [Genesis 3:17, 19]) he was able to believe in and to live a simple life.

But while natural man is basically functional, he is not basically unctional. Function is normal or natural action or use; unction is supernatural action or use. Natural man is able to function horizontally; he is not able to function in a vertical relationship with God.

Science tells us that man uses less than 10 percent of his mental capacity! What really hurts is the fact that he needs to use daily all of his original capacity but can only muster the use of a small percent. This is indeed enough to turn a brown study into a blue mood.

The Renewed Mind. The Bible tells us in 1 Corinthians 2:14, "But the natural man receiveth not the things of the Spirit of God: for they are foolishness unto him: neither can he know them, because they are spiritually discerned."

The natural or normal man is not only hampered by inability to use all of his natural mind in his daily rounds but he is also unable to move in the realm of the Holy Spirit. The divine Neurosurgeon must perform spiritual surgery to correct the effect of sin's "prefrontal lobotomy." His mind must be renewed, and the renewal of the mind can come only after the rebirth of the spirit. After the rebirth of man's spirit, the Spirit of God dwells within him.

This redemptive experience changes man's mental dimensions as well as his spiritual life. There is now a God awareness. Vertical communication is now open—the code is broken! The mind, heretofore used for natural horizontal function, is now able to lend itself to supernatural vertical unction. Previously concerned only with the things of man, he now is also concerned with the things of God.

The Apostle Paul commands the born-again Christian to have his mind renewed. In Romans 12:2 he exhorts, "And be not conformed to this world: but be ye transformed by the renewing of your mind, that ye may prove what is that good, and acceptable, and perfect, will of God."

We see here that the renewing of the mind does not come at the moment of redemption received, but that it is a following process rather than an instantaneous gift. Paul was writing to born-again, Spirit-filled Christians in Rome. If they had received the renewing of the mind at salvation, he would not have exhorted them in Romans 12:2 to receive this renewing.

A study of the verse shows the process: ". . . be ye transformed [the Greek word here is *metamorphousthe*— the process of taking form] by the renewing of your mind . . . ." (The word *renewing* in the original language of the text is *anakainosei*.) The meaning is clear as we divide the word. *Ana* means "again" in this context, while *kaino* means "new." This word tells us that the Christian mind is to be made "new again," or "made as it was before." The question that must be asked is, "Before what?" If the mind is to be made as it was "before," the answer to this question must be given.

Does this mean that the mind is to be made as it was before the salvation experience? That certainly wouldn't make sense, as that mind is precisely the mind that is in dire need of renewing. In salvation, the Christian receives the promise that ". . . old things are passed away; behold, all things are become new" (2 Corinthians 5:17). The salvation experience introduces the new, not the old; things become better, not worse.

What, then, is the "before" to which the text refers? If it is not before salvation, is it before birth? No, of course not, as we did not have a mind before birth. The answer lies in a journey all the way back through the Bible to the very beginning. Genesis chapters 2 and 3 hold the answer.

Genesis, chapter 2, tells the story of Adam's creation, his garden responsibility, his authority over the beasts, and the creation of his helpmeet, Eve. Adam's mind, not yet warped and wounded by sin, was a phenomenon indeed. Genesis 2:19 explains that God created all the beasts of the earth and brought them to Adam so that he might name them and see if he wanted one as a helpmeet. We see not only Adam's great intelligence in naming all the animals, thereby establishing human order in the garden, but we note also his discerning wisdom. Only perfect discernment would advise a lonely heart to reject every animal as a helpmeet, and turn to the Creator for a solution yet uncreated. Eve was then formed from Adam's side, and he was glad that he had waited.

Genesis, chapter 3, speaks of Eve's beguilement, Adam's disobedience, and the punishment of God upon Adam and his unborn generations. During the course of Genesis 2 and 3 something happened to Adam's marvelous mental capacity. The Scripture never again speaks of Adam's brilliance. Whether it was a combination of his disobedience and God's curse, or a gradual disintegration of his mentality, is not clear. What is clear is that the generations of Adam to this day do not possess the scintillating genius of their garden grandfather.

Before his sin, Adam communed with God on an open, person-to-person basis. There was no shame, no guile, no fear, no alienation in Adam's heart and mind. After his sin all of these positive traits were nullified, replaced by negative characteristics. Immediately, Adam began to exhibit the same kind of behavior displayed in every man today.

When Romans 12:2 speaks of the renewing of the mind or making it as it was before, it is clear that "before" refers to before the Fall of Man. God is offering the Christian an exposure to the Eden intellect. Since the institution of the sin nature, natural man's mental capability has been severely restricted. His ability to fellowship with God, as did his grandfather Adam, is as dulled as Adam's was after being driven from the garden. He lacks divine dimension. The Adamic curse is so restrictive that it can only be released through redemptive renewal. This renewal through redemption is the subject of Romans 12:2. This transformation process is begun and cultivated by the Holy Spirit for the purpose of proving ". . . what is that good, and acceptable, and perfect, will of God." Any Christian may decide to subject himself to this spiritual process, but for the Omega Man, it is not optional, it is imperative.

His Body.

> This Body is my house—it is not I;
> Triumphant in this faith I live and die.
> FREDERIC L. KNOWLES, *The Tenant*

The western songwriter said it even more graphically in his song "This Old House." The body is our earthly house, the place we live in while we are here below.

Since the Age of Reason, the Western world has put more and more emphasis and importance on the body as compared to the "inner man." The more natural or human oriented the world became, the more it became obsessed with the body. Undoubtedly, the apex of this obsession has been reached in the United States. The body has been the carnal core of Madison Avenue's advertising thrust. The partly clad female body has been employed to sell everything from swimming pools to soda crackers, from dog food to doughnuts, from cigars to car wax. The young, well-developed body, male and female, has become the symbol of physical success.

Health spas, fad diets, sixteen-year-old fashions in forty-year-old sizes, vogue hairstyles, capped teeth, toupees, implants, silicone injections, face lifts, *ad absurdum, ad nauseam,* have become part and parcel of the body-beautiful bonanza.

Never in the history of mankind has the human body received such constant curative consideration as in America in the last ten years. The average American urbanite has been examined, sedated, tested, photographed, electrocardiographed, pill fed, and measured to an extent unimagined in the days of the Great Physician.

The human body is sex symbol, idol, manikin, plaything, and medical project. It has forgotten that it is a house—a house built for a holy purpose.

The Original Owner. Genesis 1:27 teaches us that "God created man in his own image." God built the house and is the original Owner. He used divine blueprints and built it after divine characteristics and specifications. God designed it, supplied the building materials, and constructed it without flaw. But man in sinful alienation to the divine Landlord found himself a tenant in condemned property. Destruction was promised. In selfish frenzy, man began to rent and even sell his unowned, condemned property. The result was even more alienation and separation from the rightful Owner.

Then came Redemption! God, the original and rightful Owner, sent His Son to the condemnation site to buy back the property held for destruction. The price was high, some say too high. But it was paid—in full. God now owned the body twice—first by creationary rights, and second by redemptionary rights.

The born-again Christian quickly recognizes that his body does not belong to him but to God. He cannot rent, lease, or sell it, for it is not his. The Apostle Paul describes it well in 1 Corinthians chapter 6. In 1 Corinthians 6:13 he admonishes, "Now the body is not for fornication, but for the Lord; and the Lord for the body." In verse 15 he underscores the ownership of the body with, "Know ye not that your bodies are the members of Christ?" Now that the body is back in the hands of its rightful Owner, the original purpose of the Creator can be fulfilled. The human house built after His own image can now serve its holy purpose.

From Tent to Temple. From a fabric of flesh (actually no more than a tent), the human house has through redemption been refurbished on the inside. The floor has been carpeted with peace; there is laughter in the walls. The old furniture of fornication, idolatry, hatred, and wrath has been replaced with the fruitful furnishings of gentleness, goodness, meekness, and faith. And the old tenant doesn't live here alone anymore! He now has a resurrection roommate. The Landlord has sent His blessed Holy Spirit to dwell in His redeemed property.

But there is more! Its purpose has been changed! Its name has been changed! It has been changed from a residence to a rectory, from a workhouse to a worship center. The house-tent has become a temple. Paul said it dra-

matically in 1 Corinthians 6:19: "What? know ye not that
your body is the temple of the Holy Ghost which is in you,
which ye have of God, and ye are not your own?"

Verse 20 goes on, "For ye are bought with a price: therefore glorify God in your body . . . ." Earlier in this epistle, Paul introduced this same teaching with an attendant
warning: "Know ye not that ye are the temple of God, and
that the Spirit of God dwelleth in you? If any man defile the
temple of God, him shall God destroy; for the temple of
God is holy, which temple ye are" (1 Corinthians 3:16, 17).

The Boarder in the Basement. While all seems rather idyl-
lic and peaceful in this new house made sanctuary, it is not.
In the wonderful redemption process, still one very large
area has yet to be functionally redeemed—the flesh! Many
have mistaken the body for the flesh, but this is the same as
mistaking oxygen for carbon monoxide. While the house
has been in restoration, the basement has not been touched.
The flesh in its manifold manner of mischief has been a
holdover boarder in the basement. Previously it had free
run of the house. Its odor of dank, musty, self-sweat stained
every room. But the first day the new tenant moved in, a
door was installed at the top of the basement stairs. The
door bears a nameplate—it is DISCIPLINE.

Man's spirit, now reborn and rejoicing, holds the key to
the door of discipline. In Galatians chapter 5, Paul explains
the antagonism the flesh holds for the spirit: "For the flesh
lusteth against the Spirit, and the Spirit against the flesh:
and these are contrary the one to the other . . ." (Galatians 5:17). The apostle then proceeds to enumerate the
works of the flesh as "adultery, fornication, uncleanness,
lasciviousness,   idolatry,   witchcraft,   hatred,   strife,
jealousies, wrath, factions, divisions, heresies, envyings,
murders, drunkenness, revellings, and such like" (*see* Galatians 5:19–21).

These are sharply contrasted with the fruits of the Spirit, which are "love, joy, peace, long-suffering, gentleness, goodness, faith, meekness, and temperance" (*see* Galatians 5:22, 23).

The Galatian teaching continues with, "They that are Christ's have crucified the flesh with the affections and lusts" (5:24). His teaching is clear. When Christ was crucified, the dominating power of our flesh was also crucified. As we apply the purpose of the Crucifixion to pay the penalty of sin (hell), we must also apply the purpose of the Crucifixion to thwart the power of sin (flesh). The recipe for success on this Spirit-flesh face-off is found in Galatians 5:16: "This I say then, Walk in the Spirit, and ye shall not fulfil the lust of the flesh."

If the Omega Man is to be victorious, the door of discipline must be locked and guarded by the Spirit. His house of humanity has now been turned into a sanctuary of worship, a temple of trust.

Temple Maintenance. Taking care of the temple-body must be of paramount importance to the Christian. The body is an investment. It is an investment of God in man whereby God can reach man through man. Since the Resurrection, when Christ's body was raised, God has forbidden man to take the body lightly. The body is a heavenly investment in an earthly bank.

But the average American Christian is out of shape, overweight, and filled with anxieties. Many churches renounce dancing, bowling, and skating at the same time they announce banquets, potlucks, and bake sales. It doesn't take a doctor to tell us which hurts the body more.

Hardly a disease of modern history is as devastating as this corpulent curse of calories. In America the problem is pandemic. This blight of blubber has spread into almost every household. In Christian homes, it appears to be worse. It seems that the battle of the bulge has more front-line soldiers than the defense of the faith. The enemies are not difficult to identify. They represent a convenience-centered, sedentary life-style, an overconsumption of fatty foods, and an obsession with sugar.

To have a healthy body, the Omega Man must eat healthy food. Food is fuel. If he continually stokes the furnace, he could well end up looking like a potbellied stove. He must remember to eat to live, not live to eat. Fast foods are daily no-no's. Sugar should be used as sparingly as salt.

If God were to choose a modern Moses to lead the children of the church out of America into a Christian Canaan, the result would be far more frustrating than the original version. The average Christian is so out of shape that few could make it out of town, let alone all the way to "Canaan." It could take the forty years of exodus to reach the city limits. Finally, only those with automobiles and motor-cycles would be delivered.

For thousands of years man has lived by the "sweat of his brow" (*see* Genesis 3:19). His occupation insured his exercise. His normal workaday activity kept him in shape. The closer he was to the earth, the more exercise he got. Good wind, muscle tone, and a strong heart were rewards of the simple life.

Urbanization has changed all that. Man has traded his acreage for an apartment, trees for telephone poles, and pasture for pavement. He rides instead of walking. He sits instead of standing. Urban man's physical noninvolvement has paved the way for total noninvolvement. "I don't want to get involved" has become the motto of Main Street.

But God has called Omega Man to get involved. He wants to get into it all, not away from it all. He has been called of God to share, not to shun; to work, not to watch. This takes muscles and bones—strong ones. God's task is great—God's men must be fit.

How does a person get in shape? A recent United States Air Force physical-fitness study states that man is a running animal. (A running animal is a dog or cat or horse, as compared to animals that trudge, waddle, or hop.) Striding (briskly walking) and running are tremendously beneficial as regular exercise. The big three—heart, lungs, and body frame—are all exercised and strengthened. Jogging is fun as well as good exercise. Jogging for one-half hour a day, accompanied by one-half hour of simple stationary exercise, can keep the normal person as fit as the proverbial fiddle.

Keeping the temple maintained by exercise must be accompanied by sufficient body rest. Countless Christians suffer from nervousness and irritability because of an unused body and insufficient rest. The thing to remember is that exercise and rest are equal partners in the necessary daily process of recreation. It is the unused body that usually experiences unused rest. Everything else being normal, a well-exercised body will naturally seek enough sleep to make it a well-rested body. A regular diet, with regular exercise and regular rest, can make a person a regular fellow—in more ways than you can imagine.

Whether cleanliness is next to Godliness is not important, but cleanliness, too, is essential. Maintaining the exterior of the temple is as important as maintaining the interior. Being clean is a social trust, especially in America. Bad breath and body odor are inexcusable in our society. Soap must be a daily companion for the Omega Man. In short, an Omega Man should smell as good as he looks, look as good as he feels, feel as good as he lives, and live as "good" as he can.

The maintenance of the temple must be daily and devotionally attended to. It is the sacred duty of every Christian to tend the temple as the member of Christ (*see* 1 Corinthians 6:15) and the property of God (*see* 1 Corinthians 6:19).

Repairing the Temple. What if the temple is damaged and in need of repair? More than maintenance is needed. The body has remarkable self-healing abilities. It fights infection, isolates alien matter, knits broken bones, cleanses normal toxins, and sutures torn skin. Yet, there are many diseases, conditions, and injuries that it cannot self-heal. Is there healing available? If so, on what grounds? What conditions?

Do not forget the necessary world of medicine and medical doctors. However, doctors and medicine do not heal; rather, they assist the body in its healing action.

The Omega Man believes and teaches that God miraculously heals today just as he did in the Bible. Three of the touchstone Scriptures that he hangs this teaching on are:

> Surely he hath borne our griefs, and carried our sorrows: yet we did esteem him stricken, smitten of God, and afflicted. But he was wounded for our transgressions, he was bruised for our iniquities: the chastisement of our peace was upon him; and with his stripes we are healed.
>
> ISAIAH 53:4, 5

> To another faith by the same Spirit; to another the gifts of healing by the same Spirit.
>
> 1 CORINTHIANS 12:9

> Is any sick among you? let him call for the elders of the church; and let them pray over him, anointing him with oil in the name of the Lord: And the prayer of faith shall save the sick, and the Lord shall raise him up; and if he have committed sins, they shall be forgiven him.
>
> JAMES 5:14, 15

The Isaiah Scripture tells us that healing for the body is part of the redemption process. We know that our redemption is to be full and complete, lacking nothing. The Corin-

thians Scripture lists healing as one of the gifts of the Holy
Spirit to be used in the church. The Scripture in James is an
apostolic declaration that the sick ones of the church are to
call for the elders of the church to pray for healing, and that
the prayer of faith will save the sick.

These and dozens of other Scriptures give the Omega
Man great confidence in the ministry of healing. Even more
excitement is stirred when he considers Jesus' statement,
". . . and greater works than these shall he do . . ."
(John 14:12). Jesus was indicating that the miracles that the
disciples had witnessed would be surpassed in number during the upcoming ministry of the Holy Spirit. The Omega
Man believes and teaches healing for the body as part of his
faith in "the whole Gospel for the whole man." In a word,
the repair of the temple is included in the redemption of the
tent.

4

Omega Man's Priorities

In spite of his great dedication, his renewed mind, his remarkable physical discipline, and his gifted, flowing spirit, Omega Man will not reach total effectiveness until he sets and governs his life in priorities.

He is beset on every hand by demands, pressures, and emergencies. Everyone demands part of his time, part of his money, part of his dreams. Pressures mount daily. There are pressures of yesterday's unfinished tasks and to-day's seemingly insurmountable ones. Then come the emergencies. Emergencies are those unwelcome explosions that invariably are person or money centered. They demand decision and action, and they demand them now!

What does our hero handle first of the demands, the pressures, and the emergencies? If he has set his list of priorities, he knows the decisions he must make and the action he must take. Let us consider an illustrative Omega Man.

He is thirty-five, married, has six children, and is the pastor of a church. How does he choose what must be done first? How can he discern the important from the urgent? His list of priorities is revealing. He has placed them numerically according to value and importance in his life.

(1) His relationship with God
(2) His relationship with his wife
(3) His relationship with his underage children
(4) His body
(5) His mind
(6) His ministry (the church)

He has seven more things on his list, ranging from his relationship with his parents and responsibility to his community to further education at the seminary.

How and why did he choose as he did? The value judgments stand forth clearly in his rationale:

(1) *His relationship with God.* As a born-again, Spirit-filled minister of God, there is nothing so important or valuable in heaven or earth than his union and communion with his Lord (*see* Matthew 6:33; Luke 10:27).

(2) *His relationship with his wife.* He took his wife before God and men by an oath that only death can break. He is to her as Jesus Christ is to the church. The "two have become one flesh." There is no other horizontal relationship that even approaches the importance and holiness of this one. He is to love his wife as his own flesh and honor her before his flesh (*see* Ephesians 5:25–31).

(3) *His relationship with his underage children.* His children are gifts of God. He is the only earthly father they will ever know. Their early concept of the heavenly Father will be based on their relationship with their earthly father. If he doesn't care for them, he is worse than an infidel (*see* 1 Timothy 5:8). They are not his forever, but are on loan to him by God. His duty is to train them up in the way that they should go so that when they are old, they will not

depart from it (*see* Proverbs 22:6). When they are of age, they will assume full responsibility for their actions. Each likely will join with another in marriage, thereby leaving father and mother (*see* Ephesians 5:31). They then will assume the same responsibility that their parents had. When this happens, their place on the priority list must be reevaluated.

(4) *His responsibility to his physical body.* With the understanding that his body really isn't his but belongs to God (*see* 1 Corinthians 6:19, 20), and that his body is God's temple, he places his body high on the priority scale. He will, however, sacrifice his body for his Lord, his wife, and his children.

(5) *His responsibility to his mind.* His mind has been renewed by the Holy Spirit and has been reserved to think, study, and meditate on the things of God. It is the library of biblical concepts and teachings that will "guide his steps aright." He is to have the mind of Christ (*see* 1 Corinthians 2:16; Philippians 2:5). As his mind is "stayed on" God, he will exhibit "perfect peace" (Isaiah 26:3).

(6) *His responsibility to his ministry.* It may seem strange to place the ministry in sixth place. Some ministers have placed their churches and ministries above numbers two through five and found out too late that they had lost all six. A man of God must have numbers one through five in order and in concert, or he doesn't stand a prayer of being successful in number six.

Making the Priority List

Listing our personal priorities numerically is done by the examination of biblical and personal values. What is more dear to God is more dear to us. What God counts as important we must make important.

Listing priorities is a task done with an open heart and an open Bible. Notice that numbers one through five on the example priority list are relationships and responsibilities, not projects or job-success goals. Unfortunately, the latter constitute the value scale by which some people establish priorities—priorities designed, for example, to make them the president of their company, a bishop of the church, or perhaps the owner of several million dollars.

The difference in the basic philosophy of these two kinds of priority lists is evident. The first is idiographic, or person centered; the second is nomothetic, or rule-centered. The first asks, "What will it do for Christ and the church?" The second asks, "What will it do for the corporation?" The first stresses heavenly goals—relationships. The second stresses earthly goals—rewards. The first expresses the desires of God, the second the desires of man. The first holds eternal and temporal values, the second only temporal values. The first centers around the total worth of man, the second centers only around the work of man. The first speaks of others, the second speaks of me.

When one compiles a priority list, he should be certain that it is God's priority list for him, not his priority list for God!

Making Priority Decisions

Making a good priority list is one thing, but making good priority decisions is something else again. There is no threat in list making, but there is in list keeping. The establishment of priorities does not take place until the list of priorities has been acted upon.

Let's put Omega Man into a sample crisis: three of the numbers on his priority list all want him in attendance at a function, but all of the functions are on the same night.

(1) His daughter wants him to meet with her teacher on the night of school open house. It only happens once a semester, and this parent-teacher meeting is to be in lieu of a quarterly grade card. It is important, especially to his daughter.

(2) His mother and father are getting ready to celebrate important birthdays. His mother's birthday is on the eighth, and his father's is on the ninth. They always celebrate them together. This will be his mother's sixtieth birthday, more than of casual importance. To make matters worse, his sister has planned a surprise birthday party for the parents and is now on the telephone informing him of her plans.

(3) A meeting is planned at the church. While he is not directly involved in the administration of the meeting, it is generally understood that he will be there. After all, isn't the pastor on hand whenever the church doors are open? What will the people think if he is absent? Is he shirking his work?

Omega Man is in quite a predicament. All three functions are important to him and to the others involved. This is when he takes out his priority list and once again mulls over the values underlying the list's sequence.

He notes that his daughter occupies the highest position—position three. His church is represented by the sixth position. His parents have been given position number seven. His choice is clear, but it is not easy to make. Actually, the choosing is easy, it is the "unchoosing" that is hard. It always takes great courage. (By the way, many leaders fail at this very point.)

His decision is now made. He will attend the school's open house with his daughter, and notify his sister and the church of his decision. Our man has won the battle of demands—for now. He did not allow pressure to make the decision; he made it! As the months and years roll by, he will see that it was a good decision, a right decision. He has chosen the important over the urgent, the future over the present and the past.

Even though all three situations have present implications and pressures, two do not have future value. His parents find primary relationship in value past. His church duty finds primary relationship in the present. His daughter, on the other hand, along with present value, finds her primary value-relationship in the future. She is becoming what and who she will be.

Her father is an integral molder of that destiny. He has made the correct long-term value decision. He has understood that the very core of priority philosophy is the concept that present action determines future status. His decision to act or decide according to value sequence as outlined in his priority list helps him to mold what will be. His life is predicated on action, not reaction. There is no way in the world that he can react reasonably to all of the stimuli that come his way. In reaction, he can neither determine his own direction nor be the primary mover in his own involvement. He must be careful not to be the subject of Romans 12:2: "Be not conformed [fashioned according] to this world" (author's brackets). After his transformation, he is able to "prove what is that good, and acceptable, and perfect, will of God." The "transformation" of Romans 12:2 is highly spiritual, but the proving of what is good and acceptable and perfect is highly practical. It demands God-centered action based on God-given values. This is the reason for the setting of and living by divinely inspired priorities.

Perhaps you have already guessed, but if you have not, yes, our example of the thirty-five-year-old pastor with six children was a real example. What happened to him? Did his church fire him? Does his mother still speak to him?

Here are the results. He went to the school's open house
and had a delightful time. The teacher made the remark,
"Not a lot of fathers come to these conferences." His wife
was very pleased that she did not have to attend by herself.
His daughter was beaming smugly all evening long. He
couldn't tell whether it was because she was pleased that
her father attended the open house, or that she was chosen
over church and grandparents!

The church? They decided that it wasn't necessary for
the pastor to be there. After all, "He can't do everything!"

His mother and father? When the pastor called his sister
to tell her he couldn't attend the surprise party she was
planning because of the open house, she informed him that
it just wouldn't be the same without him. She was mildly
disturbed, but said she would call him later that day. When
she called, she said that a couple of the other family members also had a problem with that date, and would the following Saturday be all right? The date was open; the party
was set. That Saturday night, two days after the birthday,
the surprise party was held for the pastor's parents. It was
the only real surprise birthday party they had ever had because they were surprised two days late! It was a great
night! The pastor enjoyed it more than anyone else could
have imagined. His priority position had brought pleasure
for the present as well as promise for the future.

Some Thoughts on Priorities

Now is the time to begin work on your personal priority
plan. Open your heart and mind unto God that you see
yourself as He sees you. Use God's value system (the Bible), not yours. Don't put this off any longer. What you
postpone you actually abandon.

In Genesis, God established priorities for man (*alpha*

man—first man) that He is just now promulgating. He is
". . . the author and finisher of our faith . . ." (Hebrews
12:2).

Only the establishment of priorities allows us to plan and
project with accuracy and control. God wants man to plan
and project (*see* Luke 14:28–32). God planned and projected forward into time with perfect control and flawless
accuracy (*see* Romans 8:29, 30).

"God is not the author of confusion . . ." (1 Corinthians
14:33). A life of reaction is a life of confusion—a life out of
control!

To seek first things first is a divine imperative: "Seek ye
first the kingdom of God, and his righteousness . . ."
(Matthew 6:33).

Let us act on a prior plan (personal priorities) so that we
can ensure future fulfillment and promise.

5

The Omega Family

In the past fifty years nothing has been more assailed, demeaned, or sinned against than God's simple, holy institution, the family. It has experienced the explosion of passions and the implosion of pettiness. It has been sued, indicted, tried, sentenced, and imprisoned. It has undergone malignment, realignment, and redefinement. It has been implanted, supplanted, and replanted. It has lived in controversy, diversion, and perversion. It has been divided, subdivided, and redistributed. It has been folded, mutilated, stapled, computerized, and zip-coded. It has been uprooted, transferred, and relocated, plagued by irresponsible fathers, spoiled children, and working mothers. Sociologists call it outdated; the media exposes its seamiest sins; the young deride its established role; the church castigates its members.

Today's natural man with his natural mind would conclude that the family has an unstable past, an unworkable present, and no future.

Is it possible to go from such a morass to a miracle? Of

course it is! The One who raised Lazarus from the grave can surely raise the family from its bed of affliction! Let's set our hearts toward finding the biblical family, first by discussing what the family is *not*.

Coalition for Cohabitation

Traditional literature has carried an underlying contempt for marriage and family. There has been an unceasing and unwholesome prejudice from many of our most distinguished men of the pen. The following is testimony to this:

> The great advantage of a hotel is that it's a refuge from home life.
>
> Marry Ann; and at the end of a week you'll find no more inspiration in her than in a plate of muffins.
>
> Marriage is popular because it combines the maximum of temptation with the maximum of opportunity.
>
> Home life as we understand it is no more natural to us than a cage is natural to a cockatoo.
>
> GEORGE BERNARD SHAW

> Is not marriage an open question, when it is alleged, from the beginning of the world, that such as are in the institution wish to get out, and such as are out wish to get in?
>
> RALPH WALDO EMERSON

> O curse of marriage!
>
> WILLIAM SHAKESPEARE

> A man's friendships are, like his will, invalidated by marriage.
>
> SAMUEL BUTLER

> Almost in every kingdom the most ancient families
> have been at first prince's bastards.
>
> ROBERT BURTON

These are just a few of the multiplied thousands of references in classic literature to the inadequacies of marriage and the family. Raising our young in this climate of contempt has encouraged weeds of wonder to flourish. The young begin to wonder about marriage, their parents, and themselves. Wonder changes to wander, and wander makes its way to wantonness. Classical literature has been contemptuous; contemporary literature condemns. The family, long held in contempt, is now condemned to a lingering death from indifference and indulgence. Some new books are called contemporary literature, but they are neither contemporary nor literature. Their message is as old as Sodom, as licentious as Gomorrah. They are not literature, they are verbal VD!

Two decades ago *Lady Chatterley's Lover* was not allowed to enter the continental United States. Today it is required reading in our system of higher (?) education. Filth has been given a classification now. It is called "pornography." It can now be included in polite conversation along with biology, psychology, or even theology!

Yesterday's children are today's adults. What was read yesterday is lived today. Yesterday's literature is today's life-style. The seeds were sown and now they are grown. Old morals are passed from the scene. The sheets of the marriage bed have become tattletale gray. Divorce claims half of our marriages, and is accelerating. Is it not proper for our young to ask, "What good is marriage, anyway? Wouldn't it be wiser and easier just to live together? Can a piece of paper be that important?"

A young lady recently told me the advantages of living

together over marriage. "I've lived with three guys," she said. "When you don't dig each other anymore, you simply move out and move on—no hassle." With a small son, she was drifting through the western states in an old Volkswagen. When I asked her about the child, she said, "Oh, he's mine. I had him." The last I saw of her, she was heading for Tucson, Arizona, where, she said, "There's a family I might be able to join."

Marriage is not a convenient cohabitation without commitment or contract. It is not a sleeping arrangement between two people who "dig" one another. It is not a young lady of twenty-eight, with a chattel child and bitter memories. It is not a used-up body imprisoned in a worn, wandering Volkswagen, looking to join a family.

Marriage is the beginning of a family—a family that cannot be joined together by man, only by God.

The First Family

A Sunday-school student from a junior-high boy's class once asked me, "Were Adam and Eve legally married?" It worried him that all of a sudden they just faced each other in the garden, naked and alone! It seemed to him that somehow, without benefit of church and clergy, let alone a license, the proper ingredients of marriage were not there. I imagine these thoughts have crossed many young minds.

Another question can be added to the boy's: "Were Adam and Eve a family, or just a couple?"

Genesis, chapter 2, gives us the story of Adam without Eve, and then of Eve's creation. Chapter 3 gives us the account of their temptation, fall, and consequent expulsion from Eden.

Genesis 2:18 is an important verse, both for Adam and Eve and for us: "And the Lord God said, It is not good that the man should be alone; I will make him an help meet for him.''

Let us remember here that God's predominant concern for Adam was not his mind, his environment, his emotional and physical well-being, but his *aloneness*. God, then, by an act of creation, completed Adam as he created Eve. She was like Adam except that she was first, a female, and second, his helpmeet. Adam needed help and God gave it to him. The marriage of Adam and Eve was not in a church. No humans witnessed the rite. No legal document was signed. What there was, was God, His acknowledgment, and His confirmation. Human contracts of marriage and divorce came much later, when men needed them to keep their arrangements straight. Marriage, then, is of God initially and confirmed by men secondarily.

"Say, does that mean that one doesn't have to have a marriage license and the confirmation of the law to get married today?" Of course not, even though the law of each country is different. In fact, even our state laws are varied. We must satisfy the law to satisfy God (*see* Hebrews 13:7; Acts 23:5; 1 Timothy 2:2). Social laws are made so that man might have order, goodness, fairness, and justice. God wants us to have these same things.

How about the family question? Were Adam and Eve a family or just a married couple? They were a family. They were the first nuclear family. They were joined together by God as a family, not as a couple never to have children. Eve's name means "the mother of all living," not "wife" (Genesis 3:20). Genesis 1:28 is the proof:

> And God blessed them, and God said unto them, Be fruitful, and multiply, and replenish the earth, and subdue it: and have dominion over the fish of the sea, and over the fowl of the air, and over every living thing that moveth upon the earth.

In their loins was the family of the earth. Not just in Adam's. Not just in Eve's. But in their loins was the whole family of the earth represented. They didn't become a family when Cain was born. They were already a family. They became parents. Becoming a family was an act of creation, not of procreation. It was an act of God, not an act of man. The basic family unit is a man and his wife. This is the lowest common denominator. The smallest family is two, and the largest is ". . . all families of the earth . . ." (Genesis 12:3).

The understanding of this is of prime importance in understanding the family and its overwhelming problems. As each bride and groom marry, they are simply continuing the family of the world. But in the real, specific sense they are beginning a brand-new family. Like their grandfather Adam and grandmother Eve, in their loins rests the same potential, the same life-giving, procreative ability.

The family begins at marriage, not at birth.

The Marriage Mystery

The Apostle Paul wrote of marriage in Ephesians, chapter 5. A bachelor himself, he wrote under anointing and inspiration of the Holy Spirit. Let's examine Paul's instructions to the church at Ephesus:

> Submitting yourselves one to another in the fear of God. Wives, submit yourselves unto your own husbands, as unto the Lord. For the husband is the head of the wife, even as Christ is the head of the church: and he is the saviour of the body. Therefore as the church is subject unto Christ, so let the wives be to their own husbands in every thing. Husbands, love your wives, even as Christ also loved the church, and gave himself for it; That he

might sanctify and cleanse it with the washing of water by
the word, That he might present it to himself a glorious
church, not having spot, or wrinkle, or any such thing;
but that it should be holy and without blemish. So ought
men to love their wives as their own bodies. He that
loveth his wife loveth himself. For no man ever yet hated
his own flesh; but nourisheth and cherisheth it, even as
the Lord the church: For we are members of his body, of
his flesh, and of his bones. For this cause shall a man
leave his father and mother, and shall be joined unto his
wife, and they two shall be one flesh. This is a great
mystery; but I speak concerning Christ and the church.
Nevertheless let every one of you in particular so love his
wife even as himself; and the wife see that she reverence
her husband.

Ephesians 5:21–33

The first four verses of this passage speak of the submission of the wife to the husband. Remember, the apostle is writing to Christian husbands about Christian wives.

Verses 25 through 32 introduce a most astonishing truth—a mystery, really: The relationship between husband and wife is compared to the relationship of Jesus Christ and the church.

Seven distinct facets of the comparison are discussed in verses 21 through 33: submission, authority, love, sacrifice, cleansing, oneness or unity, and abandonment. If we seek the perfect marriage recipe, then it must be here.

(1) *Submission* (verses 21–24). One must follow. The other must lead. Submission is the first step to commission.

(2) *Authority* (verse 23). This follows point one, as submission and authority demand one another.

(3) *Love* (verses 25, 28, 29, and 33). This is the substance both of this relationship and the astounding comparison. If there is one ingredient that can stand alone, it is this one. Because it is so hard for men to comprehend the essence of

love as the essence of God, Paul gives us verse 28: "So ought men to love their wives as their own bodies. He that loveth his wife loveth himself." Where does this love come from? Is it precipitated by the object as the world would have us believe? No, it is not at all. It is precipitated by the subject. Christ loved the church! It starts with God.

(4) *Sacrifice* (verse 25). This verse reminds us that Christ gave Himself for the church. We should be further reminded that Christ gave all of Himself for the church. The command here is to love your wife, "even as Christ also loved the church, and gave himself for it." Husband love must be total and complete. We have all known the man who is suspicious and jealous of his wife, although there is no reason to be. She has to keep proving herself and her affections for him. He demands daily reassurance. He does silly things to try to gain her approval. His problem is his concept of what love is. He thinks they are still courting, and the charms of the gentle Guinevere must be won at the daily joust. He has yet to understand that he must completely sacrifice himself in love to his wife. When he does this, he will suddenly discover that she is worthy of his trust and his love.

(5) *Cleansing* (verses 26, 27). These verses are super. Paul is writing of Christ giving Himself for the church. Verse 26 says: "That he might sanctify and cleanse it with the washing of water by the word." *Sanctify* means "to set apart for a holy purpose." Sanctification presumes cleansing. A husband's love for his wife must be cleansing love. Their marriage must be set apart for a holy purpose. Marriage itself is a holy relationship and demands a constant cleansing of love. Men, do not love your wives on the merit system whereby she gains points for a clean house and loses points for a snafued checkbook. Do not remember and then remind her of her faults. Cleanse the memory of them from

your mind with the love that will present her to you without "spot, or wrinkle, or any such thing." Her desire is to be "holy and without blemish."

(6) *Oneness* (verses 30, 31). Husbands and wives are here presented a mystery. "They two shall become one flesh. This oneness, this "one flesh" kind of unity doesn't make sense in the natural, and as it speaks of Christ and the church in parallel terms in the spiritual, it is a mystery. How is it that two may become one flesh? In no other relationship in Scripture do we find these terms or this simile used. It is without question the highest form of relationship offered to mankind.

(7) *Abandonment* (verse 31). A man must leave his father and mother if he is to be joined to his wife. He must abandon any and all responsibilities and relationships that would hinder his oneness with his bride. There is no relationship under heaven, save that with his Saviour, that can hold prior claim. So many marriages are jaundiced with relationships that were not severed before the wedding. This is particularly true of mother-son relationships, and many times of mother-daughter ties. Mothers should be wise enough to untie apron strings when wedding bows are tied. *Ad majorem Dei gloriam!*

Children: Temporary Treasures

"Suffer the little children to come unto me, and forbid them not: for of such is the kingdom of God" (Mark 10:14).

Children are kingdom material. They are given to parents with blank minds and open hearts that they might be trained up in the way that they should go (*see* Proverbs 22:6). Never, as a Christian, will you be given a more precious responsibility than the training of a trusting child.

I know of a family that includes three of the nicest kids

I've ever seen. They are courteous, respectful, clean, industrious, happy, thoughtful, and beaming Christians! They are what Dr. Spock would call illegal. These qualities did not just spring up overnight like mushrooms in May. These loving Christian parents planted, watered, and cultivated each of these traits in their children. They are training up their children in the way that they ought to go.

One of the greatest needs of a small child is a good adult model. God has wisely put children in the charge of adults and not the other way around. A child needs an adult male image—a father—to follow and emulate. Likewise, the same child needs a female image—a mother—to follow and emulate. There are qualities he will need to be a complete person that only his father can teach him. His mother is needed, too, to teach him qualities that only she can teach.

William Makepeace Thackeray said, "Mother is the name for God in the lips and hearts of children." Mothers and fathers both are stand-ins for God in the lives of their children. Children are not born Christians, and must wait for that moment of God awareness for them personally that will allow them to receive the Lord as Saviour. Up until that time the parents have an added, but precious, responsibility of being in God's place in their child's life.

Parents should live with their children as people, not as wholly owned subsidiaries. A child is born with rights, privileges, and abilities. The problem is that like his body and mind, he doesn't know how to use them yet. The whole idea of putting a child into a family situation is that he will have a conducive climate in which to build his character, thus his future. God knew what He was doing.

On the other hand, it is a foolish parent who thinks that his child is a little adult and treats him accordingly. Some parents have been known to take a three-year-old into a restaurant and proceed to read the entire menu to him so that he can choose for himself what he wants to eat. They believe themselves to be fair and loving. There is no doubt about their love, but their fairness is foolish. A three-year-old should never be exposed to this kind of complex choice making. Menus have been known to frustrate the strongest-minded adults!

At his tender age eating habits and tastes are still being developed. Only nutrition-wise parents can choose for him. He will insist on choosing in a few years, and when he does, he will be able to choose wisely and well.

Children do not know what is good for them. Parents are supposed to know. Some parents do not know what is good for their children because they themselves were raised by parents who thought children knew what was good for them.

Discipline is an integral part of child training. The parent who refuses to discipline his child is cowardly and heartless. If the principles of life are not taught by loving parents, you may be sure that they will be taught by a cruel and uncaring world.

Discipline by talking only is usually not enough. If it were, we would not need our jails and prisons. We could simply reason with thieves, rapists, and murderers and tell them never to do it again. Ridiculous? Of course it is. Yet, if it doesn't work with adults, who are supposedly mature, can we expect it to work with children, who are supposedly immature? There is a rapport between parent and child that is established with a rod that cannot be established with rhetoric. Finley Peter Dunne in *Corporal Punishment* shares his humorous viewpoint:

> "Spare th' rod an' spile th' child," said Mr. Hennessy.
> "Yes," said Mr. Dooley, "but don't spare th' rod an' ye spile th' rod, th' child, an' th' child's father."

Some parents have feared that chastening a child may warp his psyche, or perhaps turn the child away from the parents in later years. The Bible does not support this opinion; it is heavily weighted in the other direction. "Chasten thy son while there is hope, and let not thy soul spare for his crying" (Proverbs 19:18). The New Testament continues the teaching in the text of Hebrews 12:6–8:

> For whom the Lord loveth he chasteneth, and scourgeth every son whom he receiveth. If ye endure chastening, God dealeth with you as with sons; for what son is he whom the father chasteneth not? But if ye be without chastisement, whereof all are partakers, then are ye bastards, and not sons.

In discipline or chastening, the rod is the method, correction the motive, and love is the mainspring! If done in fairness and love, children do not hate the parent for chastening, and as the Bible promises, the results are rich and rewarding: "But unto you that fear my name shall the Sun of righteousness arise with healing in his wings . . . . And he shall turn the heart of the fathers to the children, and the heart of the children to their fathers . . ." (Malachi 4:2, 6).

6

Four Families

Here are four case histories of families that reflect the problems of multitudes of families. Names and minor particulars of each family have been changed for the sake of anonymity.

The Green Family

John and Betty Green are faithful, churchgoing Christians. John is thirty-five; Betty is thirty-three. They have two children: Donnie, fifteen, and Diane, six.

Donnie, a very intelligent boy, is receiving below-average grades at school. He constantly argues with his mother. His best friend comes from a broken home, smokes, and rides a motorcycle. Donnie has been caught once shoplifting at the corner market.

John is worried; Betty is very worried, but hides it well. For the past six months, she has suffered from chronic headaches.

Although she is deeply in love with her husband, lately Betty has experienced a feeling of resentment toward him that she cannot explain. She works at a local laundromat four days a week, six hours a day. This allows her to get Diane off to school in the morning and get home only an hour after Diane gets home in the afternoon. She has Friday through Sunday off. She insisted on that for her family's sake. Diane is just slightly spoiled, a little plump, and watches far too much television.

John is an overachiever. He is a supervisor at a large glassmaking firm. Some say that he is the best in the company. He spends about fifty hours a week on the job. He leaves home each morning at 6:30 A.M. and gets home about 5:30 P.M. He also works three nights a week from 7 to 10 P.M. at a local office, doing tax consultation. He and Betty attend a neighborhood Bible study each Thursday night. John is also president of the Homebuilders Class at church. The first Friday evening of every month, a planning-and-prayer session for the class is held at the Greens' home. The third Friday of every month is the Homebuilders Class party at a member's home. The first and third Saturday mornings of each month are spent at the Full Gospel Business Men's breakfast.

John is getting tired. His back is starting to bother him, and that extra twenty pounds—will he ever lose it? He is worried about Donnie. "Kids just aren't the same anymore." And Betty is beginning to act funny—kind of cold—sometimes. *What's wrong with everybody? I'm doing the best I can!* he thinks.

Some Thoughts for the Greens. John is a man suffering from doing too many things, and doing them out of priority sequence. He is doing the most he can, but he isn't doing the best he can. Donnie has been wounded by a scanted father-son relationship. John is well on the way to losing his son, if he hasn't already done so.

Betty, worried about Donnie, too, has worried herself

into chronic headaches. They started just after the shoplifting incident. Diane seems to be growing up like a weed in a window box.

What can be done to help?

Help must start with the father. John must stop right where he is and rework his priority list. He must put his wife and his children before work, church, Bible study, the Sunday-school class, and the Full Gospel Business Men! Suggestions are that:

(1) John reorder his priorities.

(2) Give up Bible study on Thursday night to spend the evening with Donnie in a crash effort to reestablish a relationship.

(3) John and Betty make another crash effort to get out of debt as quickly as possible so that John can cut down or cut out the night job.

(4) Betty readjust her hours at the laundromat so that she can be home when both children leave for school and return from school. Their house needs to be turned into a home.

(5) John ask about working with the high-school department at church instead of the Homebuilders, so that he and his son could be involved at church together.

(6) Every Saturday night made a family night with dinner, fun, and reading from the Bible. It would be a great preparation for Sunday.

(7) With their doctor's okay, the family should begin to jog together three days a week. (Don't knock it 'til you've tried it!)

The Lewis Family

Maxwell and Roberta Lewis are as different as night and day. Their life has been a comedy of errors. It started at the

wedding when she hurt his neck by bussing him too en-
thusiastically.

Maxwell is not yet forty-two; Roberta is forty-three.
Roberta is a charismatic Christian, gloriously gung ho and
gifted. She is about thirty pounds overweight, but has more
energy than a troop of Boy Scouts. She is outgoing in every
avenue of her frenetic life. She loves to minister in the gifts
of the Spirit, especially the verbal gifts. This penchant for
using the gift of tongues at almost any opportunity, plus her
bionic thyroid, makes her downright terrifying to neophytes
and Baptists.

Maxwell is a Baptist—a Southern Baptist. He is very
thin, very bald, very quiet. Roberta and Maxwell have a son
named Waltham. (He was named after Roberta's father, but
Waltham takes after his own father: he is a fourteen-year-
old Maxwell.) Waltham is a straight-*A* student, and has the
largest stamp collection in the city. He rarely leaves his
room after supper except to go to Pentecostal fellowship on
Sunday nights, which he hates.

The problems of this family are not leading them to divorce court, or for that matter, even to a marital tiff. The
biggest of their problems is the absolute absence of recip-
rocal personal interchange between husband and wife.
Maxwell is so passive and so outgunned by the mere presence of his wife that his offering to the marriage relationship
is little more than his weekly paycheck. In their rare intimate times, impotence results from intimidation.

Roberta is positive that all Maxwell needs is the Baptism
of the Holy Spirit—and Pow! All will be well. She is wise
enough to know that he will not go forward in any public
meeting. Therefore, she buys him books and cassette tapes
on the Holy Spirit. She's done this for almost ten years.
Maxwell may well have more books and tapes on the Holy

Spirit than Oral Roberts. As of this date, nothing spectacular has happened. What can be done for this marriage?

Some Thoughts for the Lewises. It is evident that neither Maxwell nor Waltham will make it big in Toastmasters International. However, the problem of Roberta's wild-horse personality running roughshod over her husband and son can be solved. She is so immersed in her own religious experiences that she is insensitive to where her husband and son are spiritually. It is apparent that they will not respond to the gifts of the Spirit, but they are starving for the fruit of the Spirit.

Here are some suggestions:

(1) Roberta must bring her high-octane personality under control according to the dictates of Galatians, chapter 5.

(2) She must lose the extra thirty pounds. She would lose much of the overcompensation drive, and would look better and be more healthy. It couldn't hurt in their intimate moments, either.

(3) She should have her bionic thyroid checked by the doctor.

(4) She should quit purchasing books and tapes for Maxwell, and give the money to Waltham for stamps.

(5) She should spend an evening a week with Waltham and his stamp collection.

(6) She should attend church with Maxwell instead of vice versa.

(7) She should obey Ephesians 5:22: "Wives, submit yourselves unto your own husbands, as unto the Lord."

Pam Henderson and Children

Pam is twenty-eight years old. She has been divorced for two years. Her husband, who had been having an affair with a woman at his office, left her about three years ago. There was one very nasty year as charges and countercharges were hurled back and forth.

The last two years have been more peaceful, but they have been hard and they are getting harder. Pam has a naturally sunny disposition—one her friends say is getting a little more cloudy a little more often. There are three children. Freddie is eight, quiet, nervous, and fearful. Julie is six and is the all-American girl. She is naturally ebullient and joyously happy. She is the *deja vu* of her mother. Kevin is three, loud, wild, and rough. It was during Pam's pregnancy with Kevin that her husband's affair was discovered and the information relayed to Pam.

Pam's troubles are prolific and pressing. They are emotional, physical, financial, and increasingly mental. The children so need for her to be home, and they need a daddy. Freddie was never gregarious, but he has grown nervous and fearful over the past few months. Pam thinks he has taken the place of the man of the house, and emotionally it is destroying him. Kevin needs authority, but Pam is too tired and emotionally hungry herself to discipline him after a long day at work.

"Work! Why is it so hard now? I used to breeze through four hours of dictation standing on my head!" Pam's musings are becoming more and more centered on herself. "I'm so darn lonely! George is so kind and thoughtful." (He's her next-door neighbor.) "Why do I find myself looking at him so often? I really should start back to church. People . . . they ask so many questions . . . . What . . . just what in the world am I going to do?"

What can Pam and her three children do? We have already established that the lowest common denominator in the formation of a family unit is a husband and a wife.

Pam's husband is gone. The family is now a broken family, an incomplete family. There is no way in the world Pam and the children can continue as a family as if nothing has happened. If marriage is a bicycle, then one of the wheels is gone. She had always been the back wheel. She didn't steer, she just followed along. Now she is a unicycle. Riding a unicycle, especially with three kids, is a most difficult endeavor.

Pam has tried to place a male image closer to the children by having her father come over and take the children out once a week. It has not worked. He has been more like a "Godfather" than a grandfather.

The whole financial picture is shaky, also. It is really difficult to make the payments on the house. Neither can she keep up a four-bedroom house and work. It is just too much.

Some Suggestions for Pam.

(1) Start back to church immediately. The strength and communion of her spiritual family is needed.

(2) See about getting a Christian "big brother" for Freddie, perhaps a brother from the body of the church.

(3) Sell the large house and move into something that can be handled.

(4) Get out of debt. Use the ten-year equity money and the money gained by inflation on the house.

(5) Start a social life; seek out a Christian parents-without-partners group.

(6) Start a daily devotional time with the children. The evening is the best time.

(7) "Be strong and of a good courage . . ." (Deuteronomy 31:6). Pray daily for strength and courage as one with the responsibility of two.

The Banduci Family

Richard Banduci is twenty-nine. Lois is thirty. They are Christians. Both of them made decisions for Christ as teenagers. They have been married for nine years. They have no children. Richard has a good job with better-than-average pay. He has been in his job for ten and one-half years and is well liked. Lois did not work until about three years ago, when she became bored with their one-bedroom apartment. It was during this time of boredom that Lois began to collect pets. The first pet she acquired was a chicken. It started off very innocently as a little chick at Easter. "He was so cute, and so tiny!" He is not tiny anymore. He is not even a he! Her name is Frances. Frances has since been joined by Poo Poo, the cockapoo; Hamilton III, the turtle (two others died), nicknamed "Hurryin' Hamilton"; and a yellow bird, called "Yellow Bird."

Her going to work gave the Banducis even more financial mobility. They have a new sports car and his-and-her Porsche driving jackets. Much of their money is spent for clothes. Either one could qualify for clotheshorse of the month.

As for their church affiliation, it is smug and not taxing. They attend two different churches in the area. One was hers before they were married, the other was his. They have relatives at both. Attending two churches is advantageous in that there is no real commitment involved at either. Besides, if they are too tired to go some Sundays, the folks at one church think they are at the other.

Richard and Lois love each other. They seem to have a carefree, *Vogue* magazine life. They apparently have beat the system as far as church is concerned. Financially, they are floatable. What problems could they have? Are there any thorns in Eden?

Richard and Lois live in a general atmosphere of dissatisfaction and unfulfillment. McDonald's Farm has not been a good substitute for children. Their Porsche jackets don't look as well on them as on people ten years younger. They have so many clothes that new clothes are unsatisfying and disappointing. Their beat-the-system church relationship is no relationship at all. Neither fellowship feels that they are part of their family. The purpose and goal of life that they held nine years ago does not seem to fit anymore. Although they seem to have the most of life with the least of responsibility, they are depressed.

Richard and Lois are caught in the trap that has caught so many young couples today. Their only commitment is to each other and fulfilling each other's fleshly desires. Their commitment to other people, to God, a church, and an everlasting goal is weak. Fulfilling the desires of the flesh has been disappointing. They must reach beyond themselves. They must reach out! They must reach up!

Some Suggestions for the Banducis.

(1) Set down and establish a godly goal for their lives.

(2) Sell the "farm," or at least thin out the stock.

(3) Join one church—maybe a completely different one. Commit themselves in giving, attendance, and serving it.

(4) Stop buying clothes for at least six months.

(5) Trade the sports car in for something more suitable to their new commitment.

(6) Give their Porsche jackets to their just-married new neighbors.

(7) Consider a new Banduci—either having a baby or adopting one.

Extra Family Preparations

Because of the unique times in which we live, we have unique problems we must face on the family level. The signs of the times point to the fact that we are entering into a last-day culture. We have been immersed in a superindustrialized society that has been production and convenience oriented. Each one of us depends more and more on people and organizations we do not know to supply us with the necessities of life—a nice convenience as long as we can depend upon those who supply us. Today, when we have become more dependent than ever, the ones we have depended on have become less and less dependable.

It is time for Christian families to take stock of just how self-sufficient they really are. How able are we to care for ourselves and those around us in a national crisis or even a local emergency? At a time when we will be needed most in helping and ministering, will we be a help or a hindrance? Will we be as unprepared and helpless as children in a school yard, or will we be ready to help and to minister the Gospel in practical, everyday terms? Christian families should be prepared for the things that must come to pass (*see* Matthew 24:6), so that the bride of our Lord Jesus will be fully prepared for the One who must come. Let us get our house in order.

Get Out of Debt. Never was "Owe no man any thing, but to love one another . . ." (Romans 13:8) better advice than it is today. Living unnaturally high, way above our proportion of need, is a common deadly practice. Too long we have been bound by the chains of our own self-indulgence to a financial philosophy of a little bit down and a little bit each month.

This seemingly harmless practice has sown the seed of financial irresponsibility throughout our country as thoroughly as a farmer sows wheat. We are dollar bound. Many have sold their future for the next two to five years to the same creature that devoured New York—credit! As Christians, we cannot afford to make most of our decisions based on finances. They must be based on faith. It is impossible for us to have faith for our future if our future has been mortgaged to the hilt. Strike the devil a real blow by getting out of debt.

Mend Your Family Fence. So many families are divided by squabbles and strife. Maybe it is a mother and daughter who are not speaking, or a father and son who do not see eye-to-eye. Some husbands and wives carry on a continual cold war. Now is the time for us to forgive one another and join our families together in love. The hour is late and the times perilous. We are to work until our Lord comes. We are to wait for His appearing. Let us work and wait together—as a family—full of grace and love.

Return to the Pantry Principle. From the Garden of Eden until fifty years ago, we lived by the pantry principle, the providing of food for our family according to the seasons. God gave us the seasons, and they haven't changed. Spring is for planting. Summer is for growing. Fall is for harvest. Winter is for resting the earth. Between God's built-in natural preservation of various foods and our own methods of preservation, we have learned to keep our food through its cycle. In fact, today we can keep it through several food cycles.

Yet, what is happening? We have turned over this basic responsibility to others. We have become so urbanized that we do not even control our own food cycle. Here again, we are depending upon a system that is becoming less and less dependable.

What can we do about it? Shall we all take up farming

again? No, aside from a home garden, that wouldn't be possible or desirable. To maintain a year's supply of food on hand—from harvest to harvest—would be simple. All it takes is a little planning, dedication, and some work. A few families have been doing this for some years now. If an emergency arises, they are ready. If nothing ever happens, they are ready. It is a great feeling to eat today at last year's prices. They can put the difference into the Lord's work. What an easy way to give more than their tithe.

Someone once asked, "What if there was a national emergency, and we couldn't get food at the market. What then if somebody came to your house to demand food?" He went on, "Would you get a gun to protect your pantry?"

I said, "My goodness, no. I would help him carry it to his car!"

How wonderful it would be for us to have something to share!

> Go to the ant, thou sluggard; consider her ways, and be wise: Which having no guide, overseer, or ruler, Provideth her meat in the summer, and gathereth her food in the harvest.
>
> PROVERBS 6:6–8

All in the Family

The family is the nucleus of civilization.

WILL AND ARIEL DURANT

The family is one of God's most important gifts to the world. In the day of unprecedented pressures on the family we must protect what we have now, and prepare for the more ominous days ahead.

Each member of the family has a personal obligation toward this end. Fathers must become fathers, and mothers become mothers. Both need to be less occupied with role playing, more involved with the responsibility of parenting and partnering. Children, too, have to find a place of purpose and primacy in the family.

Each member of the family should be planning, preparing, and participating together. A family is nothing if it is not first a relationship of reliance and respect by each member for each member. When a family begins to function in faith toward each other and toward God, then the Bible's promise of complete fulfillment will be experienced by all in the family.

7

The Church: What It Was, and What It Is

At the outset, I beg the reader's indulgence, and in apologia, ask for acceptance of the method I have used in dealing with the church, historic and present.

Satire is the best literary vehicle to use for a painful subject. If you look closely, you may observe tears in the midst of tee-hees and grief among the guffaws. Perhaps the old sarcastic adage has merit: "It only hurts when I laugh!" I want it to hurt! I want it to hurt deeply! So, laugh with me. Laugh as long as you can.

The History of the Church

Charles Merrill Smith has given us a succinct and satiric history of the church in *The Pearly Gates Syndicate*. "We call it the 'Pearly Gates Syndicate,' " he says, "because the product it purveys is admission to heaven, real estate in paradise, assured entrance through the pearly gates."

Considering that many today suggest the impending demise of the church, let us take a quick look backward at some of the roots of our syndicate.

Apostleship: "Avon Calling!"

Although we have unbounded enthusiasm and respect for the Early Church apostles, they were, by and large, losers. They came, in the main, from society's lower echelons. Their educational qualifications were, at best, suspect. Their business acumen was nonexistent. Their organization was bad, their public relations were worse, and their advertising program abominable. Their product promotion was acceptable, but it was probably more luck than largess. Their junior-executive program met with little success, as did the profit-sharing plan. Most of the administration was left to Peter and an imported "headhunter" from Tarsus named Paul.

It is fitting and proper for us to hold the apostles in reverence, but for us to imitate their methods would be corporate suicide. It is too bad that our first executive directors could not have read Dale Carnegie or Norman Vincent Peale! It would have done wonders for their confidence.

The Christian Corporation

After almost three hundred years of the Early Church somehow bungling its way from one success to another (antiestablishment all the way!), it reached a point of corporate necessity. Constantine was saved, and he wanted everybody else to have what he had (whether they wanted it or not).

Under Constantine the church became a corporation (the Pearly Gates Syndicate). It left its antiestablishment position and became proestablishment. "You can't fight city hall!" was its motto.

The change in attitude paid off handsomely. Whereas it had been gauche to be a Christian in precorporation days, it was now chic, definitely the "in" thing. From this moment on, in church history the performance of pope, parson, or penitent must be evaluated by the rules and guidelines for General Motors (amen)!

Pecking Order Established

In the early days you could scarcely tell the clergy from the laity. But this was not good corporate strategy. By its very nature, a corporation has a hierarchical structure. We must know who pecks whom, and by whom and from whom pecks are to be received. Without an organizational ladder, how would we climb to corporate heights?

Although there is some disagreement on just who pecks whom on the lower end of the ladder, the rungs usually follow this pattern: First we have bishops (preachers). After the bishops come the elders (deacons), and following the elders come the deacons (elders). Next in line are the song leaders (would-be or have-been preachers), then the head usher (would-be or has-been military general). Last comes the church janitor (would-be anything else). This kind of structure, confusing as it seems, gives everyone a sense of belonging and well-being. It also provides someone to share the blame. Sharing the blame is very important in the Christian corporation.

Don't Steal My Sheep

It wasn't until the sixth century that we developed the parish system. Individual churches were given a prescribed territory in which they were to "preach the gospel to every creature" (Mark 16:15). Boundary lines were carefully drawn so that local churches would know just how far to go.

(Or how far not to go?) Overseeing bishops (some denominations call them district superintendents) were responsible for the delineation and administration of each parish. The decision to divide the world into parishes was just what the Christian corporation needed to establish its grass-roots organization. It made the corporation executives look good, too, as it provided for:

(1) A fair and equal opportunity for each local dealer.
(2) A system to regulate sheep stealing.
(3) A way to convert pagans at the lowest possible cost.

This was terribly important, as the young corporation was beginning to get involved with expansive building projects, new, expensive foreign markets, and, of course, escalating administrative costs.

This seems to be a good time in which to share the first verse of the Christian corporation song (sung to the tune of "Onward Christian Soldiers"):

Christian Corporation, marching to the bank
Doing Christian business, hear the money clank;
Success our ruling passion, power our greatest prize,
In the name of Jesus, who can criticize?

Chorus
Christian Corporation, moving to the top
Holy Aspirations! nothing us can stop.

Charles M. Smith, we thank you.

Breaking Up the Monopoly

Until the eleventh century the Christian corporation was enjoying unparalleled success. There were small problems here and there, but the corporate ink blotter absorbed them. But now the syndicate was to suffer its biggest threat to date. The power block from the East (holding stock options galore) had decided to split the corporation. The Western block did all it could to keep the corporation intact, to no avail. In 1054, the Christian corporation split into the Roman (Western) corporation and the Orthodox (Eastern) corporation.

We will say, to the credit of both Eastern and Western corporation executives, that the division was caused finally over the most weighty of matters. It had nothing to do with some of the previous conflicts over baptism, the Trinity, or salvation. No, the Pearly Gates Syndicate split over the great picture controversy, or, "Shall we or shall we not have pictures in the board room?"

Go Now, Pray Later

The icon controversy and the Eastern split notwithstanding, the Middle Ages saw the Western corporation grow in power and influence. In fact, it grew so strong that it needed to flex its corporate muscles more. For hundreds of years Christian-corporation executives had fretted over the fact that the Holy Land was ruled by unholy people. The place the corporation held as sacred and venerable needed liberating from the grasp of the infidel. The corporate order was issued. Memos were distributed. Horses were shod and swords were sharpened. The Crusades were on!

After two hundred years of Crusades, led by an assortment of kings and knights, even children and a hermit, the corporation's enthusiasm for crusades began to wane. As a business venture, they were a bust. The home-office executives decided to regroup and spend some time and money on the corporate image. Oh, well, *Deus vult!* ("God wills it"—the rallying cry of the first Crusade.)

Edifice Complex Takes Shape

The Gargoyle often makes his perch
On a cathedral or a church
Where, mid ecclesiastical style,
He smiles an early-Gothic smile.

OLIVER HERFORD

The Early Church in its precorporation days gave very little thought to buildings. Somehow, it muddled along from house to house with only a message and the anointing of God.

As a millenium had come and gone, however, it was now time to think of home, image, and tall buildings. "After all, God has blessed us so. Shouldn't we build a great building where we may worship and He may live?" (Heretofore, God had been allowed to move freely about the community, but from now on, He was remanded to the custody of the cathedral.)

Just like that, the "edifice complex" was born, and Gothic architecture was to become a Christian-corporation trademark. Although the style is different today, the "edifice complex" still lives in even broader Babylonian dimension.

Gothic architecture was just perfect for the corporation's new image. It was high and mighty, very heavy at the top, with shaky walls held up by outside supports (flying buttresses), and with windows that were too small to see in or out. (Some say that the corporation was as Gothic as the architecture!)

How did the poor people of the Middle Ages raise all that money with which to build the local "Gothic Glory"? Five "tired" and true methods were used:

(1) *The special rich list.* A secret list was made of all the

rich members of the congregation and community. They were then visited by the finance committee. They were not approached in this manner because they were rich—oh, my, no—but rather because "they were such good Christians."

(2) *Memorial windows and furniture.* Even though Gothic windows were nonfunctional as far as light, air, and vision were concerned, they became financially very functional. Someone thought of the idea of making the windows out of little pieces of colored glass, and gluing the pieces together with hot lead. Someone else said, "Let's make pictures and designs with the little pieces of glass!" But the real genius was the one who said: "Let's sell these windows to help build the church!" Thus the memorial window was born.

It was such a blessing! You could give to God and have your name in colored lights at the same time. After the memorial windows, it didn't take long to spread the blessing to the altar furniture and various other blessed bric-a-brac.

(3) *Emotional appeals after a heavy mass.* As most giving is like most buying—emotionally initiated—this was a highly prosperous method. (As the bishops of the twentieth century are so much more advanced and sophisticated in the use of this method, I'll not embarrass the Gothic clergy by any further discussion.)

(4) *Selling heavenly favors.* This was a fire-insurance policy with an escape clause. The premiums were high, and the benefits somewhat suspect. The fine print was impossible to read. It had all kinds of calendar problems, too, concerning such things as when you go to hell and when you get out and when you go to heaven and how long you can stay.

(5) *Gifts from the laity* (Bingo came later). To build a great cathedral, a great financial base had to be established. All the little people were asked to pony up. Gifts were

received from craftsmen, farmers, soldiers, and servants. The only unacceptable gifts were from "public sinners." (Gifts from private sinners were cheerfully received.)

Luther—the First Protestant

Martin was a monk-priest in a little German town about the beginning of the sixteenth century. He had been rather unsuccessful in finding meaning to his life through the Christian corporation. After many years of prayer and soul-searching, he decided that the element of personal faith was missing. The Pearly Gates Syndicate did not supply this kind of faith, being more predisposed toward corporate faith than individual faith. Also, at this time the "selling of heavenly favors" had grown to preposterous proportions. There was leaven in heaven.

Martin, feeling strongly about the situation, decided to advertise. He nailed his ninety-five "gripes-and-statements" list to his church door. This began a reaction that got Luther tried, convicted, and thrown out of the corporation. He then formed a small business on the side. Martin's business was so successful that it encouraged others to take this "step of faith" and do the same. Before long, there were more Lutherans, Presbyterians, Baptists, Methodists, and other assorted Protestants than one could shake a stick at.

The Corporation Discovers America

In 1492, the corporation's advance man, Christopher Columbus, discovered America. The theme of discovery for the New World was "God, gold, glory" (probably not in that order).

Never in the checkered history of the Christian corporation was there a greater conquest! America was a great prize. She was rich in natural (and, yes, supernatural) resources. Religious freedoms were provided and encouraged. Money was printed with imprimatur of godly trust. Her government would monitor morality and pray before parley. The very foundation of government would be laid along godly guidelines. Here, for the Christian corporation, was a brand-new field, the opportunity of the ages. Here was a land that in less than twenty decades would be the glory of nations, past and present. What should be done with this awesome responsibility?

The American Brand

Things began rather slowly but with admirable equanimity with our Pilgrim forebears. Churches were established in accepted patchwork fashion throughout New England. This was a serious brand of religion. Stark was smart, and Spartan was special. Reds and yellows were worldly. Blacks and grays were heavenly. Fear was in, fun was out. Guilt was heavy and forgiveness elusive. Life was death and death was life. Trust was as scarce as children at chore time. Works were imperative, while grace was a premeal prayer. "Fun time" was the Sunday-afternoon reading of *Pilgrim's Progress*—family style (a feat still unequaled in modern penance, with the possible exception of home movies).

The stage was set for a Great Awakening. It began in the early 1700s. The flames were fanned into roaring revival in 1741 by a sermon delivered by Jonathan Edwards. His "Sinners in the Hands of an Angry God" brought fear to the boldest hearts. Each syllable was saturated with sulphur, each sentence was a gavel of judgment. Terror, stark and Styxlike, stalked the aisles. Pews became penitential pyres. Strong men came screaming to the altars. Women fainted on the way. The Great Awakening was on! The corporation was establishing a Christian consensus.

This was the spirit that spawned the American Revolution. The middle and late 1700s are some of the most cherished years of America's history. Dedication, integrity, courage, and God-awareness were common man-on-the-street characteristics.

The nineteenth century dawned with great expectancy and optimism. Thomas Jefferson was elected president of the United States. He possessed genius and intellect not seen in the presidency before or since. The nation was moving from the cradle to the playpen. In the next fifty years, it would move from the playpen into the neighbor's yard to fulfill its Manifest Destiny.

What about the church? Where was it during this time? Many of the churches were tired of the Puritan ethic and its negativism. Sectional cultures and social changes were threats to the old way. The question of North versus South, free versus slave, and a multitude of attendant controversies needed to be dealt with. Grandfather's church was stifling and inflexible. Many wanted to "go over the wall," to escape the Puritan penitentiary.

The Plan to Ignore Hell

The middle of the nineteenth century witnessed the birth of American liberal theology. Liberalism's greatest voice at this time was Henry Ward Beecher. Henry had gone "over the wall" and sought a place of greater expression. He felt that love should be preached instead of fear. He had tried the old way without success. In three years of strong Calvinistic polemic, his preaching, he said, "did not make a single sinner wink."

He reasoned that his generation was interested in art, business, politics, and how to have fun. He reasoned correctly, for the sheep began to flock to his church. It was while Beecher was pastoring the Second Presbyterian Church of Indianapolis, Indiana that he polished up his new pulpit approach. He preached on controversial cultural topics that drew crowds to the church. Topics of little cultural interest, such as drunkenness, Sabbath breaking, and gambling, were also included. The subject of hell was at first ignored, then abolished altogether as a completely untenable topic.

Later, Beecher would accept the pastorate of the Plymouth Congregational Church of New York City. Here, he would establish himself as the bishop of American liberal theology. (Thank you, Henry. You made sin acceptable and hell unacceptable. Theology became much more sophisticated from then on.)

From Mules to Machines

The end of the Civil War marked the beginning of great change in America. The North was grasping for production. The South was grappling with destruction. The time clock of progress, which had always been slow in the South, was now turned back even further. Having historically been ninety-five percent agriculture and five percent industry, she now, torn by war, was not ready for any fast changes. The South would, in weak and wounded fashion, continue its agriculture-based existence for a while longer.

In the North, it was a different story. Factories, geared for war production, were now ready to continue with peacetime products. New machines were needed. Men created and patented them by the thousands. New ideas, new products, new machines, new factories—and the cycle repeated itself over and over again. The Industrial Revolution was on! Men were turning from mules to machinery, from agriculture to industry, from the country to the city. America had entered a new age. It was an end of an era for the church, too.

Even though the Civil War had reunited America politically, the religious division remained. There were still Southern Methodists, Presbyterians, and Baptists, and Northern Methodists, Presbyterians, and Baptists. The splitting of denominations along the Mason-Dixon line was only the beginning of the corporation's necessary strategy for the new involvement. New churches were started by the thousands as the country continued to move west. As the number of churches grew, the importance of denominational clout intensified. District and national headquarters were established and then expanded. (The Christian corporation pretty much followed the history of General Motors; there were Buick Baptists, Pontiac Presbyterians, Chevrolet Congregationalists, and so forth.)

There were splits in the various denominational divisions, as well. For example, the Baptists insisted on their "right to fight" at the monthly business meetings, and fight they did. Before long, there were more than a dozen separate (and autonomous!) Baptist brands from which to choose. By the turn of the twentieth century, each major denomination had expanded, consolidated, and split. (Sounds ambiguous, you say? Only in America could this kind of ambiguity be called progress!)

The Twentieth Century—"Bullish on America"

By now, things were really moving! The next sixty years would give the American Christian corporation more members, more buildings, more money (more splits), in general, more clout. The Pearly Gates Syndicate's (American Division) finest hour (dividend speaking) was at hand.

Bigger and more beautiful church sanctuaries were built, greatly facilitating the care of the widows and orphans, not to mention the poor! Great new educational buildings and programs were launched. (Great idea, but about 1900 years late—actually, only 150 years late for American Christians. Americans are never as late as the rest of the world.) Established seminaries were enlarged, and their faculties lionized. (Holiness developed an IQ.) Bible schools and Christian colleges spread like mononucleosis at a love-in. Radio became the ego extension of small-town preacher personalities, assorted Elmer Gantrys, and even legitimate Gospel ministries. The Christian star was born! Television would later make him a superstar.

Competition between local franchises (churches) grew to National Football League proportions. Building the largest sanctuary, the biggest membership, the highest steeple became obsessive. The paranoia of the "edifice complex" turned on the church while turning off the world. Church architects and interior decorators were respected and better paid than church missionaries. (Missionaries are those slightly strange professionals selected to go into all the world to preach the Gospel while we stay home and pay for the new carpet in the choir loft.) It is all put into perspective with another verse of the corporation hymn:

> Onward Christian soldiers, marching as to war,
> Carping, fighting, splitting, as we did before.
> Buying carpets, windows, organs, and a silver bell
> While the world around us marches off to hell.
>
> *Chorus*
> Onward Christian soldiers, we're building to the sky,
> We'll build a higher steeple than the other guy!

The American Christian corporation was riding high. The market was bullish; denominational Dow-Jones averages were impressive, and the big board in the sky winked its neon approval.

8

The Seven Churches of the Corporation

Today, the Christian corporation has sophisticated its methodology of churching into seven different franchise approaches. Methods were the result of years of experience in sales and promotion. The strategy was foolproof. (Hardly any fool could prove it!) It was comprehensive, covering conservative, liberal, and a middle-of-the-road approach.

Church Number One: The Parish Church

This church is not going anywhere. It is happy with where it is. It is orthodox (old) and conservative (theologically, politically, and methodologically—if perchance not in the first two, most assuredly in the last!) It puts a premium on membership and regular church functions. It tends to be exclusive rather than inclusive. The pastor is expected to conform and confirm, not to initiate and integrate people or programs that differ from the status quo. The mission of this church is to reach the reached.

107

Church Number Two: The Evangelistic center

This is a very fundamental body. It is Bible oriented,
contending that every book in the Bible is inspired equally.
However, most of the sermons come out of John, Romans,
and the Epistles, giving us the impression that some books
are more equal than other books. These folks like to mark
and chart in their Bibles with colored pencils (John and
Romans will be marked considerably, while Matthew and
Acts are pristine black and white.)

The main exercise of this church is "witnessing." This is
sometimes called "soul winning" or "getting people
saved." This is usually accomplished by one or more of the
following:

(1) *Personal witnessing.* This is an individual effort and
one of the hardest. It can be done at work or at play. Because the individual must feel "led" as to time, place, and
target, this is the most mystical of the three methods. Usually, only people who are "a little strange" socially are any
good at it.

(2) *Witnessing teams.* A minimum of two is required here
(no maximum—the more the merrier, the less the scarier).
The tools for this endeavor are a Bible (preferably Scofield),
a stout heart, and a memorized sales talk. The goal is to get
as many people as possible to "pray the sinner's prayer,"
thereby getting "saved." The number of fish caught will be
remembered and "testified" about at a later church service.
Most of the "fish," regrettably, do not find their way into
the local communion, as follow-up is difficult and unfulfill-
ing. (Everyone knows that it is more fun to catch fish than it
is to clean them.)

(3) *The evangelistic meeting.* This is the most popular
method of "winning the lost." The "unsaved" are invited
to a church service (usually to hear an ex-gangster, dope

addict, or someone with a similarly disreputable past). The Gospel is then presented in fervent yet hygienic fashion. The end of the service is reserved for the "altar call" or decision time. No one is allowed to go to the altar before the altar call, as that is against the rules. Actually, everything is done in rather apple-pie order. Adults find this method of witnessing more desirable as it is less personal, thereby less frightening (to the Christian, not to the sinner!). Personal witnessing is more for the young people, as they haven't experienced enough to be afraid.

The evangelistic center spends so much time in evangelizing that there is scarcely time left for the poor, the widow, the orphan, the homeless, community needs, or local government. (Oh well, "This world is not my home, I'm just a-passin' through.")

Church Number Three: The Once-a-Week Worship Experience

Most often this is a liturgical service. (Follow the printed menu.) Quality is the theme. (One hour a week doesn't qualify for quantity.) The sanctuary is beautiful, spacious, and comfortable. The windows are stained and leaded. The fountain in the narthex sends semiholy water cascading in a glorious gurgle over a pastoral scene depicting the Shepherd's Psalm. The rest rooms are located to the left and to the right of the narthex. The men's rest room is done in subdued and dignified beige tones. The women's rest room is considerably larger and more graciously appointed than the men's. (Men rarely complain about rest-room facilities.) Beautifully coordinated furniture is arranged in an area dominated by a golden wall mirror. (This is for last-minute repairs. If one is only going to spend an hour a week with God and His people, one had best look worthy.)

When the service starts, it is inspiring. The choir and

clergy, appropriately robed, march with dignified grace to their prescribed positions. (Robes always demand an entrance.)

The Invocation is delivered (a pontifical preparation in the second and third person, designed to offend no one, including the devil).

The choir is presented. (It sings only songs by men who have been dead a long time, preferably those whose names begin with *B*.)

The offering is received (in velvet bags, by ushers who never look to see how much is put in).

The homily is delivered. (The parish church calls it a sermon. The evangelistic center calls it a message. Other people call it other things.)

The Benediction is submitted (welcomed by all).

The pipe organ plays a lively recessional (Bach's musical account of his persecution and ultimate demise).

The family beautiful rises from the beautiful cushioned pew, smiling beautifully at other people, passing through the beautiful sanctuary into the beautiful narthex, by the beautiful rest rooms, through the beautiful copper-inlaid outer doors, into the parking area that is beautiful in white line and nursery planting. What are their thoughts after such a beautiful service?

> *The Son:* "I've got to get out of these monkey clothes."
> *The Daughter:* "Who was that new guy sitting with the Johnsons?"
> *The Mother:* "That wig of Gloria Mandate's is just about the brassiest red I have ever seen!"
> *The Father:* "At last! A smoke!"

What a beautiful worship experience. Just beautiful.

Church Number Four: The Bible-Study Fellowship

This is a very conservative, Bible-centered church. The Bible is the textbook, the pastor is the teacher, and the people are the students. The church building is the classroom. The church does not have to be beautiful, but it has to be functional. If it can manage both, all the better.

The pastor-teacher is usually in one of two categories. He will be classical or he will be casual. He will be Dr. George Biblestudy, or else he will wear turtlenecks and go by his first name. Either way, he must have a marvelous three-month study on Revelation, preferably with attendant chart. He must also be an expert on the Old Testament, with the ability to find Zephaniah on the first try. He must be scholarly, but not professorial, wise but winsome, and well prepared yet warm. He will seek to punctuate his lessons with his own brand of humor, being careful to avoid the hilarious and the hokey.

The laity of this church are different altogether. They do not possess the soul-winning fervor of the evangelistic center. They can sit in church longer than the people at the beautiful church, although they won't look as pretty. This church could, with reasonable success, find the minor prophets, while the folks at the beautiful church have a hard time finding a Bible each Sunday to carry to church.

The folks at the Bible-study church also know the difference between a carry Bible and a study Bible. At the drop of a proverb, they will tell you the difference between a "Dakes," a "Dickson," and a "Tommy chain." With no further encouragement they will also give you an opinion on the "Living," the "N.A.S.," and the "Amplified." If you are still around, you will receive briefs of the "Berkeley," the "R.S.V.," and the newest paperback interlinear.

The pastor's Bible will be color coded for chain-subject

reference, with green for prophecy, blue for history, red for eschatology, and various assorted colors for various assorted themes. The greatest pleasure you can give him is to let him show you a verse in Habakkuk, completely surrounded by colored-in verses, ball-point-pen notes, and his own cryptic hieroglyphics. (Ah! The ultimate in Christian one-upmanship!)

The church as a Bible school often fosters a doctrinal exclusivism that smacks of a ''We know what it's all about, but you don't'' attitude. They have also been accused of ''always going to Bible study, but not doing anything'' (a ''hearers of the Word only'' indictment). When more experience-oriented groups accuse these folks of neglecting prayer, praise, and worship for Bible study, a verse will be shown in defense to counter this accusation.

Church Number Five: The Church in Revolution

''We will overcome!'' is the cry of the social-action church. There are problems that must be addressed, wrongs that must be redressed, and established concepts that must be undressed. (This dressing business is a full-time job, so they leave prayer, Bible study, and soul winning to the other churches.) This is the most liberal stance of all of the seven churches. The entire mission of the church is to change the status quo (Latin for ''the mess we are in''). ''Let us cut down the well-manicured hedgerows of the Establishment, and plant a new garden: one without weeds, one without thorns. A garden where everyone can be a flower.''

Those who attend this church have dedicated their efforts to changing society. A common mark of dissent has been to grow a beard so as to look different in a beardless society. (As this is generally difficult for female dissenters, they usually wear their dissent in the form of stringy hair.) Dissatisfaction with the status quo is also shown by wearing sloppy clothing and hillbilly shoes. This kind of clothing used to look dirty, ill fitting, and unkempt, but is now accepted as modish, in vogue, and fashionable. Anyone now can buy new sloppy clothing and new hillbilly high-top shoes. And one can wear them with pride. People now know that you wear them because you want to look modish, in vogue, and fashionable, and not because you have to. The problem with everybody wearing them is that now it looks like assent rather than dissent.

Another way that social-action church members express dissatisfaction with the Establishment is to make up songs, play the guitar, and sing. (Few pianos are used, as they would hinder the mobility of the revolution.)

Perhaps the greatest manifestation of dissatisfaction is the freedom march. (It is common among dissenters to feel that they are in bondage to something and must be freed.) A good freedom march has tremendous benefits. Good, fresh air and exercise, along with meeting new friends, are not the least of these. If the march is big enough, the press and police always show up. (The Establishment pays for the publicity and the protection.)

What is sad is that those who sing "We shall overcome" do not realize that Jesus Christ already overcame. The perfect community, the utopia that they are seeking, is part and parcel of the package of redemption. Our freedom march was made over nineteen hundred years ago by One who walked the *via Dolorosa* to the place where all changes are made—spiritual, physical, and yes, even social.

Church Number Six: The Weekly Emotional Release

Some churches act as Gospel group-therapy sessions. They are solely experience oriented. Woefully weak on

Bible knowledge or a sense of world evangelism, they seek
to translate God into personal (emotional) experience only.
Special "preaching" voices are used. Prayer is publicly
given in the minor key. Singsong phrases and statements
demanding a response are issued from the pulpit. Exagger-
ated hand clapping and soulish beat music are employed
with a "work 'em up" fervor. Musical instruments of all
sorts of pedigree, and special vocal numbers add to the
dissonance. Before long, the physical and emotional move
as one, both out of control. The meeting continues until
weariness winds down the participants. When they leave to
go out into a world of need, they are too drained to disciple,
too spent to serve.

These churches offer little or nothing in the way of educational or social programs. They are strictly meeting
oriented, and spend their time, money, and strength toward
this end. It is well said that they "produce a lot of heat, but
not very much light."

Church Number Seven: "My Kingdom Come"

The Lord promised us that we would live and reign with
Him in His kingdom. However, this seventh church of the
Christian corporation is building its own kingdom here and
now. It almost always starts with a man—a man who is
strong in personality, determination, and leadership. He
begins to build, and he builds buildings and more
buildings—buildings for worship, for school, for media, for
programs, for projects. The programs are large, the projects
varied.

The worship sanctuary is the largest in the city, perhaps
in the area (the Pharaoh complex). He doesn't trust existing
school systems, so he builds his own. He will be media
oriented—in radio and/or television. He will continue to

erect and build until his name or initials will somehow subscript his statement of mortar.

Alexander Pope (1688–1744) helps our understanding in his *Moral Essays:* "Who builds a church to God, and not to fame, Will never mark the marble with his name."

This strong man assumes a self-imposed apostleship status to the surrounding church community. His words become superecclesiastical and extrabiblical. (Even he finally begins to believe that he is something special and must be treated accordingly.) Many follow his leadership as he appears at once bold, gifted, exciting, and strong.

The size and function of his kingdom attracts as many as his personality does. His kingdom spreads his message. His message is a strange admixture of God words, optimism, veiled promises, and suave deceit. (He speaks as he does everything else, with great flair and distinction.) His ever-expanding kingdom becomes the platform for his ever-increasing ego.

Finally he is his kingdom, and his kingdom is he. The ministry has become the man. Observe this latter-day prophet—for he is a prophet, a false prophet. ("Let him who has ears to hear, hear what the Spirit is saying unto the churches" [*see* Revelation 2:17]).

Where Are We Right Now?

Leaving the vehicle of satire, which we used to muscle our way by mirth and no little misery through nineteen hundred years of church history, let us now consider the problems and promises of today.

From the turn of the twentieth century until about 1960, the churches of America flourished in everything one could count. Memberships, attendance, baptisms, and offerings increased yearly. In the violent sixty's, denominations,

both major and minor, began to stall and lose altitude on
their growth charts. There were exceptions, of course, but
in general the church scene was sick. As the seventy's
dawned, it became sicker still.

Today the church is weaker than ever. The weakness
cannot be measured in numbers only. Its message is weak,
its leadership cowardly, its vision fuzzy and myopic. Its
virility has been drained away by self-indulgence, its morality compromised by the harlots of humanism. It has become
more earthly than heavenly. Where once it was a sweet-
smelling savor unto the Lord, it is now a stench in His
nostrils. Someone has said, "The church today is like
Noah's Ark: if it wasn't for the storm on the outside, you
couldn't stand the stench on the inside."

In the first century we saw the triumph of the spiritual. In
the twentieth century we are now experiencing the triumph
of the secular. Elmer Towns, in his book *Is the Day of the
Denomination Dead?*, speaks of this:

> Perhaps it is too late to stop the influence of secularism
> in the American society; maybe the mainline denomina-
> tions have passed the point of no return and a mercy-
> killing is justified. If so, the only hope in the future is the
> raising up of new super-aggressive churches that have
> returned to the original mystery of Christianity. These
> churches can answer man's dilemma through the super-
> natural.

Secularism has not so much diluted the image or program
of the church as it has decimated the people of the church.
As Charlie Shedd has plainly said it, "The problem is not
that the churches are filled with empty pews, but that the
pews are filled with empty people."

What is going to happen to these empty people and the

empty world that they have been commissioned to win? Men, even good men, godly men, have fallen short of answering this question. We have quoted for years that "man's extremity is God's opportunity." Today, man appears to be in extremity. Does God have a plan, a strategy for a last-days church that He is ready to unfold? Is it the renewing or "greening" of the existing church, or is it something brand-new and different?

What is it that we are to expect from God? Can some kind of superchurch be the answer? If not, what can stand and flourish in the chaos of change that we face? What could be that flexible, that mobile? What could be strong enough to reach an unreachable world, a world that is populating faster than the historic church at its strongest could ever convert? What is peaceful and loving enough to keep people who are suffering intense stress and strife from attacking one another? Is there an answer?

9

The Church: What It Should Be

Although there are a variety of ways to launch a discussion of what the church should be, one proven technique is to state concisely what it should not be.

This last-day church must not be a success as the world views success. How large, how many, and how rich must not be the measuring sticks of God's glory. The church that is built by man's specifications, encompassing man's goals, and employing man's function, is a church by man, of man, and for man.

The specifications, the goals, and the function, as man, are temporary. Worldly success is based on the American triumvirate of competition, victory, and reward. God's kingdom has no room for competition. Business flourishes on competition. Sports are based on the competitive. But the free Gospel of Jesus Christ denounces competition and instead demands cooperation. The church of Jesus Christ must not take direction from Madison Avenue or Wall Street, but from the street called "Straight" and the road called "Calvary."

118

The Omega Church: An Overview

Since God is working out His *alpha* or original purposes in these *omega* days through the Omega Man and the Omega Family, it must follow that His Omega Church pursues these purposes. This last-days church must literally reflect God's original purpose and power. It must manifest the wisdom of Proverbs, the inspiration of Psalms, the power of the Acts, the teaching of the Epistles, and the mystery of the Revelation. Its character must be pure and holy, its message simple in presentation but profound in power and application. A method that is scriptural and spiritual must be coupled with preparation that is comprehensive and extensive.

The Omega Church must dissolve all boundaries—denominational, national, geographical, and so forth. This church must not limit its parish to streets and communities, but extend its ministry to seas and continents. It must not be wholly Baptist or Methodist, or solely Presbyterian or Catholic; it must be wholly and solely Jesus Christ's.

The Omega Church must concern itself with the hungry and the thirsty both physically and spiritually. It must build buildings that are at the same time practical, flexible, and ministry oriented. This church cannot yield to the temptation of constructing costly cathedrals. It must dedicate its tithes and offerings to ministry, not to mortar. This church must have the ministerial mobility and agility to respond to the daily beck and call of the Holy Spirit.

The Omega Church Character

The character of God's church should speak of the character of God. The Bible teaches us that God Himself dwells with us (as born-again Christians) in the Person of the Holy Spirit (*see* 1 Corinthians 6:19). The Holy Spirit

molds the character of each believer according to the will
and character of God. The results of this character building
are found in Galatians, chapter 5. They are called the "fruit
of the Spirit." There are nine fruit listed in Galatians 5:22,
23. They are love, joy, peace, long-suffering, gentleness,
goodness, faithfulness, meekness, and temperance. The
first three are the key. If you possess a full measure of love,
joy, and peace, the remainder will follow.

People everywhere seek love, joy, and peace, but find
only sorry substitutes. Love, joy, and peace cannot be won
or worked for; they are not fruits of labor, but fruit of the
Spirit. They cannot be attained or achieved; they are the
property of God for the provision of His people and the
province of His church.

The development and manifestation of the fruit of the
Spirit for God's people and God's church is a command
from God Himself. It is the fruit of the Spirit that holds the
line against the works of the flesh (*see* Galatians 5:16–21).
The Omega Church must possess and express the fruit of
the Spirit. The world must see, hear, and feel the love of
God, the joy of God, and the peace of God. The church of
the last days must manifest this fruit to the unbelieving
world as well as to its own church constituents. To possess
love and not express it is a sin! The same holds true for joy
and peace. Let's manifest the fruit of the Spirit, the root of
our character, for all the world to witness.

Love is manifest in giving: "For God so loved the world,
that he gave . . ." (John 3:16). Joy is manifest in praise.
Psalm 100 instructs us, "Make a joyful noise unto the
Lord . . ." and to come ". . . into His courts with
praise . . ." (verses 1, 4). The Prophet Isaiah follows with,
"Sing, O heavens; and be joyful, O earth; and break forth
into singing . . ." (Isaiah 49:13). Peace is manifest in righteousness (holiness): "The fruit of righteousness is sown in

peace of them that make peace" (James 3:18). "And be renewed in the spirit of your mind [peace]; And that ye put on the new man, which after God is created in righteousness and true holiness" (Ephesians 4:23, 24, author's brackets).

For the Omega Church to live in the daily exhibition of love, joy, and peace is not an easy task. God never promised love without rejection, joy without sorrow, and peace without pain. Yet, it is precisely these kinds of trials that prove the truth of God in the affairs of men.

Let us express and exhibit the love of God in an open and free manner, and do it in purity and boldness. How do we start? A church in Dallas, Texas, started by having a holy, hugging time every Sunday morning in the middle of the worship service. People were instructed to seek out and hug ten other people. The pastor and all the congregation became involved in this simple, spiritual expression of love.

The Omega Church Message

The message of the church must be fourfold in application. Each of the four areas must be centered in Jesus Christ. Christocentricity must be the hallmark of each and every message coming from the Omega Church.

Jesus Christ: Our Saviour. The Bible says that "all have sinned, and come short of the glory of God" (Romans 3:23). It goes on to declare, "For the wages of sin is death; but the gift of God is eternal life through Jesus Christ our Lord" (Romans 6:23). The Apostle John teaches, "For God so loved the world, that he gave his only begotten Son, that whosoever believeth in him should not perish, but have everlasting life" (John 3:16). John further explains, "But as many as received him, to them gave he power to become

the sons of God, even to them that believe on his name"
(John 1:12).

We see, then, that all of us have sinned, and we fall short
of God's glory, but God has given us the gift of eternal life
through His Son Jesus Christ. Christ died to pay the penalty
for our sins. If we believe Him, and receive Him, He will
give us the power to become His children.

If you have never asked our Lord Jesus Christ into your
heart and life, why not stop right here and pray, "Dear
Lord Jesus, I'm sorry for my sin. Come into my heart and
life right now and cleanse me, and make me perfectly
whole. Be the Lord of my life and teach me Your ways.
Amen."

This message of Jesus Christ as Saviour is the most important message that we can preach. Without the realiza-
tion of Jesus Christ as Saviour, all other messages are
meaningless.

Jesus Christ: Our Baptizer in the Holy Spirit. Each of the
first five books of the New Testament has a verse that is
essentially the same. The verse promises that Jesus Christ
will baptize His followers in the Holy Spirit (*see* Matthew
3:11; Mark 1:8; Luke 3:16; John 1:33; Acts 1:5).

The initial occurrence of the Holy Spirit baptism was on
the day of Pentecost (*see* Acts 2:2–4). At this time the Apostle Peter and all of those who were tarrying in the upper
room were baptized in the Holy Spirit. They had been ex-
pecting something, but they weren't sure just what. Jesus
had promised them a new, spiritual power that would come
after this Holy Spirit baptism (*see* Acts 1:8). And the power
did come! They were powerful in preaching and
witnessing—in fact, so powerful that three thousand souls
were added to the church that very first day. Later on in the
Book of Acts, we see that God wanted Gentile believers to

have this same baptism. Through the use of a heavenly vision, the Lord arranged for Peter to go down to the house of Cornelius, a Roman officer. As Peter was sharing the message of God with Cornelius and his household, the Holy Spirit fell on them even as He had on Peter and those in the upper room (*see* Acts 10:44–47).

Through the last nineteen hundred years of church history literally millions have been baptized in the Holy Spirit and have received power from on high. Even in America's brief history, there have been several outpourings of the Spirit. The charismatic movement which began in the 1950s is the latest of these Spirit outpourings. Now, in these times, we are witnessing the greatest of Holy Spirit movements. But it has just begun! We are truly experiencing the fulfillment of Joel's prophecy:

> And it shall come to pass afterward, that I will pour out my spirit upon all flesh; and your sons and your daughters shall prophesy, your old men shall dream dreams, your young men shall see visions: And also upon the servants and upon the handmaids in those days will I pour out my spirit.
>
> JOEL 2:28, 29

The Omega Church needs power to minister in these last days. The power comes from God through the Baptism of the Holy Spirit.

Jesus Christ: Our Great Physician. Is there healing in the blood of Jesus Christ? The answer is a most emphatic yes! One of the least understood teachings of the Bible is the subject of healing. Consider this question: If Jesus' ministry was so full of healing, why doesn't the church teach and practice the ministry of healing more than it does? Some have answered, "That was Jesus' own personal ministry, and was not meant for His followers." This, of course, as it stands contrary to Luke 9:1, 2, cannot be.

> Then he called his twelve disciples together, and gave
> them power and authority over all devils, and to cure
> diseases. And he sent them to preach the kingdom of
> God, and to heal the sick.

We see conclusively that a large part of the disciples' ministry was healing the sick. Some have quickly countered, "Yes, His disciples were given this power, too, but that was still part of Jesus' earthly ministry." This position does not follow the progression of Scripture, either. In the Book of Acts, long after Jesus had departed to His Father, thereby ending His earthly ministry, the disciples are still healing the sick. In fact, Peter is used on a much grander scale in healing than he ever was during Christ's earthly ministry.

The Book of Acts also tells us of the powerful healing ministry of Paul, who was not one of the twelve, had nothing whatsoever to do with Christ's earthly ministry, and, as far as we know, never saw Jesus in person. Someone could argue, "Yes, but Paul was an apostle, with all the attendant apostolic gifts and power. We are just regular, garden-variety Christians." However, Paul, in his first letter to the church at Corinth, writing to garden-variety Christians (chapters 1 through 6 prove this), teaches them of the gifts of the Spirit for ministry, and healing is among them.

Later, the Epistle of James goes one step further and buttons down the ministry of healing as a required local-church ministry: "Is any sick among you? let him call for the elders of the church; and let them pray over him, anointing him with oil in the name of the Lord: And the prayer of faith shall save the sick, and the Lord shall raise him up . . .'' (James 5:14, 15). James then continues with, "Confess your faults one to another, and pray for one another, that ye may be healed" (verse 16). We must conclude that the ministry of healing is not only a legitimate but also a required ministry for the church today.

Is healing of the body part of Christ's redemptive work? The answer is again an emphatic yes. Isaiah promised it, and later Christ confirmed Isaiah's promise. First, let us look at Isaiah's promise:

> Surely he hath borne our griefs, and carried our sorrows: yet we did esteem him stricken, smitten of God, and afflicted. But he was wounded for our transgressions, he was bruised for our iniquities: the chastisement of our peace was upon him; and with his stripes we are healed.
>
> ISAIAH 53:4, 5

These verses plus the rest of chapter 53 most assuredly speak of the Crucifixion of our Lord. But what about the word *healed* in verse 5? Does it mean spiritual healing only, or is there a broader application? The answer comes several hundred years later during the earthly ministry of Jesus. The text and context are found in Matthew, chapter 8. Most of the chapter is involved with healing.

At the outset, Jesus healed a leper who had come to Him for that purpose. Next, a Roman centurion approached Him to see if He would heal his palsied servant. After declaring the faith of the centurion and the healing of his servant, Jesus went to Peter's house. Peter's mother-in-law was laid there, "sick of a fever" (verse 14). Jesus touched her and healed her.

When evening had come, many were brought to Him for ministry: "And he cast out the spirits with his word, and healed all that were sick" (verse 16). Now watch closely as

we add the next verse (17): "That it might be fulfilled which
was spoken by Esaias the prophet, saying, Himself took our
infirmities, and bare our sicknesses." Notice that Jesus
translated Isaiah's "borne our griefs" into "bare our
sicknesses," and Isaiah's "carried our sorrows" into "took
our infirmities." There is no doubt that Jesus Christ is not
only fulfilling Isaiah's prophecy as to physical healing, but
is also confirming its message into New Testament terms
and authority. Matthew 8:17 verifies that Isaiah 53:4, 5
speaks of physical healing.

There is healing for the body in the blood of Jesus. Jesus
Himself said so. And the capstone of confirmation is found
in 1 Peter 2:24:

> Who his own self bare our sins in his own body on the
> tree, that we, being dead to sins, should live unto righ-
> teousness: by whose stripes ye were healed.

Who would know better than Peter what Isaiah had
prophesied and Jesus had verified? It was at Peter's house
that Jesus explained the passage!

A note of caution: Let us not get so carried away with the
fact that healing for the body is in the Redemption that we
overlook the primary thrust of Isaiah 53: healing for the
spirit. The body is only temporal, while the spirit is eternal!

Jesus Christ: Our Returning King. Jesus Christ is now at
the Father's right hand, but He will return for His bride, the
church. He has gone that He might prepare a mansion for
her (*see* John 14:2). In the following verse Christ explains,
"And if I go and prepare a place for you, I will come again,
and receive you unto myself; that where I am, there ye may
be also" (John 14:3).

He will come in great glory! Matthew 24:30 tells us, "And

then shall appear the sign of the Son of man in heaven: and then shall all the tribes of the earth mourn, and they shall see the Son of man coming in the clouds of heaven with power and great glory.''

Jesus will come quickly. Paul is speaking in 1 Corinthians: ''Behold, I shew you a mystery; We shall not all sleep, but we shall all be changed, In a moment, in the twinkling of an eye, at the last trump: for the trumpet shall sound, and the dead shall be raised incorruptible, and we shall be changed'' (1 Corinthians 15:51, 52).

His coming will be dramatic:

> For the Lord himself shall descend from heaven with a shout, with the voice of the archangel, and with the trump of God: and the dead in Christ shall rise first: then we which are alive and remain shall be caught up together with them in the clouds, to meet the Lord in the air: and so shall we ever be with the Lord.
>
> 1 THESSALONIANS 4:16, 17

He will return to set up His kingdom without interference from Satan (*see* Revelation 20:1–7). He will be the King over His kingdom forever and forever (*see* Psalms 10:16).

There is controversy today as to just when Christ will return. Some think it will be before the great tribulation period spoken of in the Book of Revelation. Others still are satisfied that the great tribulation period must come to an end before Jesus Christ returns. These positions are known as pretribulational, and posttribulational.

It seems small to make any of these eschatological positions a test of fellowship. Matthew 24:36 clearly states: ''But of that day and hour knoweth no man, no, not the angels of heaven, but my Father only.'' It is time we quit tussling over terms and splitting over speculation. Perhaps the old farmer was right after all when he called himself a "pantribulationist." He was not sure what he believed concerning the time of Christ's return, so he just reckoned that it would all "pan out" in the end.

The Omega Church must not become embroiled in such nonedifying issues, but must spend its energies in fulfilling Christ's command concerning His return: "Occupy till I come" (Luke 19:13).

The Omega Church Method

The Omega Church method is simple, direct, and powerful. Do everything in the guidance and power of the Holy Spirit. The Old Testament speaks of a legal approach to God. This is called nomothetic, or "rule centered." The New Testament teaches a personal approach to God. This is called idiographic, or "person centered."

The legislation of the Old Covenant could not bring life, whereas the New Covenant is based on the Person of Christ, who is "the way, the truth, and the life" (John 14:6). We, then, are debtors, not to the law, but to the life that is in the Person of Christ. Paul said it strongly in 2 Corinthians 3:5, 6:

> Not that we are sufficient of ourselves to think any thing as of ourselves; but our sufficiency is of God; Who also hath made us able ministers of the new testament; not of the letter, but of the spirit: for the letter killeth, but the spirit giveth life.

This New Covenant was not instituted just to initiate life for the life receivers (Christians) and then let them revert back to the Old Covenant approach. Christ is not the life spark that gives man the wherewithal to now keep the rules and regulations of the Old Covenant. We do not start with

Him and then continue with the law, but we start with Him and continue with Him. He is "the author *and* finisher of our faith" (Hebrews 12:2, author's italics). The Galatian church was having this precise problem. Paul admonished them with:

> O foolish Galatians, who hath bewitched you, that ye should not obey the truth, before whose eyes Jesus Christ hath been evidently set forth, crucified among you? This only would I learn of you, Received ye the Spirit by the works of the law, or by the hearing of faith? Are ye so foolish? Having begun in the Spirit, are ye now made perfect by the flesh?
>
> GALATIANS 3:1–3

The Galatians, as many in the church today, began in the Spirit, but then tried to turn their idiographic relationship into a nomothetic one. We cannot use the law of Moses as the General Motors' method of perfecting the things of the Spirit. Only the Holy Spirit perfects the life in the Spirit.

Our church must not be characterized by the rules of the nomothetic, who seek personal conformation. Instead, we seek general confirmation of the Holy Spirit by a method of ministry that is person centered and, consequently, life giving.

There is a Spirit-filled church that is really trying to do all things under the guidance of the Holy Spirit. It truly is successful in every area except one: finances. This church is using financial formulas of the world. It hired a full-time money raiser, but he just cannot seem to raise enough money. Each month this church falls deeper and deeper into financial chaos. "O foolish Galatians, who hath bewitched you, that ye should not obey the truth . . . having begun in the Spirit, are ye now made perfect by the flesh?"

Another Spirit-filled church in the same state as the one

just mentioned is also trying to do all things under the guidance of the Holy Spirit. It truly is successful, too, in every area, including finances. Each week the pastor shares openly with the people, and together they take the need to God. There is always more than what is needed! This church does not receive late notices on any of its accounts, and has an A-1 credit rating in the community.

It's not only in finances but in every area of church function that we need to flow in God's Spirit. Give me a church usher who manifests the fruit of gentleness and temperance, and I will give you a church usher who has a vital ministry in his church. The same holds true for each task in the church where the fruit of the Spirit are manifest.

The fruit of the Spirit tells just half of the story. The Omega Church must discover, develop, and use the gifts of the Spirit resident in the congregation. Ephesians 4:7 declares: "But unto every one of us is given grace according to the measure of the gift of Christ." These "grace gifts" are given to every one of us. (Do you know what your gift is?)

Later, in this same chapter, Paul enumerates and explains the "office gifts": "He gave some, apostles; and some, prophets; and some, evangelists; and some, pastors and teachers; For the perfecting of the saints, for the work of the ministry, for the edifying of the body of Christ" (Ephesians 4:11, 12). These gifts were not given to every one of us, but to some of us.

In 1 Corinthians 12:7–10, Paul talks about the "manifestation gifts." These gifts of the Spirit are divided into three categories:

(1) The Mouth Gifts
    (a) Prophecy
    (b) Divers Kinds of Tongues

    (c) Interpretation of Tongues
(2) The Mind Gifts
    (a) Word of Wisdom
    (b) Word of Knowledge
    (c) Discerning of Spirits
(3) Ministry Gifts
    (a) Faith
    (b) Gifts of Healing
    (c) Working of Miracles

The context of this chapter makes it clear that each Spirit-filled Christian is given at least one of these gifts: "The manifestation of the Spirit is given to every man to profit withal" (verse 7). However, verses 28 and 29 teach us that all members of the body do not have all of the gifts. To whom are these different kinds of gifts given? They are not the exclusive dominion of a professional elite, but they are given to the body. Everyone in the body is to be gifted. All three categories of gifts, the grace gifts, the office gifts, and the manifestation gifts, must be represented and exhibited in every local church.

The Omega Church must have as its method of ministry the moving of the Holy Spirit throughout the congregation. The Holy Spirit must be the initiation, the continuum, and the completion of all projects. Life must be ministered every day and in every way, from parishioner to pastor, from custodian to choir member. In short, we must share the fruit and use the gifts!

The Omega Church Parish

The parish of the Omega Church is the world. The Great Commission given to the church by Jesus Christ was, "Go ye into all the world, and preach the gospel to every creature" (Mark 16:15). The Father loved the world (*see* John

3:16), and Jesus died for the world. Going "into all the world" is the continuation of God's concern. It is the vision and perspective of God, not man. Don't you think it strange that Jesus would give this commission to men who probably had never travelled more than one hundred miles from where they were born? In the eyes of man it would appear presumptuous and peculiar, especially considering that the speediest transportation in those days was a galloping horse. But God has a world vision that fits His world love and world redemption. We must have the same vision for the world that God has.

How can we do this? How can we practice what we preach? There are four actions we must take:

(1) *Let us go ourselves*. With the world as small as it is because transportation is as fast as it is, we can go! The Omega Church must be a mobile church. People of the church must actually go out in ministry throughout the world. Yes, it can be done; in fact, it is being done right now. A church in California has within the last year sent ministry teams (church members accompanied by a pastor) to New Zealand, Australia, England, Ireland, Scotland, Guatemala, and Yugoslavia. Plans for next year call for even more countries. First-time decisions alone have amounted to fifty times the number that were made in the local church itself. The same pastors and the same people who attend the local fellowship are directly responsible for fifty times the ministry of salvation at home base!

(2) *We can send*. We can send people, money, supplies, and know-how. After the devastating earthquake that hit Guatemala in 1976, this same church sent all four! Food and clothing and emergency supplies were gathered by the truckload. Thousands of dollars were collected. Craftsmen of the church accompanied the money and supplies that were sent to missionaries for distribution. The Christian

craftsmen worked on building construction and repair in the daytime, and ministered in tent evangelism at night. It was one of the brightest hours the church has ever had.

(3) *We can care.* One of the most-often-voiced complaints of missionaries is that people at home just don't seem to care. Recently a church sent some money to help reopen a Bible school in Australia. Word was returned that the school was going to open on a certain date. The church sent a telegram of congratulations and mutual excitement to the school officials. They were overjoyed! Someone cared! Sometimes little things are more important than big ones.

"The world" does not have to be a foreign country only. The ends of "the world" may be China or Australia, but the beginnings are right outside our church doors. In a western city a little Baptist church was having some serious financial problems. In the same city, a Pentecostal church, hearing of the dilemma, took up an offering for the sister ministry. With great surprise and thanksgiving, the money was received. There is now a tight bond of love and cooperation between the two churches.

A group of Christians was visiting the Holy Land. One of the group noticed that some of the hills had trees growing on them, while adjacent hills were barren. The Israeli guide told him that almost all the trees had been cut down as punishment by invading armies of the past. The guide went on to explain that the government of Israel was now involved in a massive reforestation project. Moved by this, each of the Christians bought an olive tree to plant near Jerusalem. The Israeli guide was touched; someone cared!

Perhaps it is not possible for us to go, but we must care. The Omega Church is a sharing church—a caring church.

(4) *We can pray.* All the world needs prayer. Let us be a people of prayer. We can change the world and its course through prayer. We must pray in four dimensions. First, we

must pray *specifically*. Matthew 21:22 says, "And all
things, whatsoever ye shall ask in prayer, believing, ye shall
receive." In other words, we get just what we ask for in
prayer. If you pray for a used car, don't expect a new one.
Let us learn enough about the people and places we pray for
that we may pray intelligently and specifically.

We must pray *continually*. We should quit the punctilio-
production kind of praying and continue steadfastly in intercession. We must follow David's declaration:
". . . prayer also shall be made for him continually . . ."
(Psalms 72:15). We can fasten our hearts to the object of
prayer and continue until the prayer has been answered. We
must "pray without ceasing" (1 Thessalonians 5:17).

Then, we have to pray *fervently*. James tells us, "The
effectual fervent prayer of a righteous man availeth much"
(James 5:16). The English word *fervent* comes from the
Latin word *ferveo*—"to boil." We must get hot in
prayer—hot enough to boil! Then we continue to boil until
the Lord releases us from that responsibility.

We must pray with the *Spirit*. There comes a time when
our mind and mother tongue are inadequate to pray as we
ought. Paul states this clearly in Romans 8:26: "Likewise
the Spirit also helpeth our infirmities: for we know not what
we should pray for as we ought: but the Spirit itself maketh
intercession for us with groanings which cannot be ut-
tered." Being filled with the Holy Spirit enables us to pray
in this fashion. Later, Paul speaks of this again: "For if I
pray in an unknown tongue, my spirit prayeth, but my understanding is unfruitful. What is it then? I will pray with
the spirit, and I will pray with the understanding also" (1
Corinthians 14:14, 15).

It is a surety that as Alfred Lord Tennyson said: "More
things are wrought by prayer than this world dreams of."

10

The Omega Church Prepares

Someone has said, "Preparation is not fun, but it is necessary." It's not a popular word in this day of instant gratification.

We are offered prepared foods, prepared fun, prepared fashions. We have little patience for preparation in our convenience culture. We instantaneously acquire ready-mades and "already dones." Our suntans are sudden, our hobbies half-assembled. Our food is precooked, our clothes are pre-shrunk. Our health is prescribed and our thoughts are "pre-thunk." Know-how has been unionized. Social ability and cultural expertise preclude personal ability. We live in a prepared society. The question is, "Prepared for what?"

We are not prepared individually or corporately for ministry in these days and the days to come. The things that we daily find prepared for us do not prepare us. The more *last* the days get, the more personal and urgent the responsibility becomes. The more our society prepares things for us, the less we know of preparing things for ourselves.

Even the practice of handing down skills through the family from one generation to another is rarely honored today. The most common form of this, found in mother-daughter traditions of cooking and sewing, is not so common anymore. How many young brides do you know who can cook and sew with any proficiency? The bridegrooms are in the same boat. They possess a lot of general cultural and social knowledge, but little personal specific knowledge. If they do not join the hordes of eight-to-five cliff dwellers who hang by their financial fingernails from Monday 'til Friday, they have little chance of making it.

It is plain that we are prepared only for more of what we have been receiving; we have not been prepared at all for the end-time experiences that are even at the door.

Let us as Omega People prepare for life and ministry for these great days! Let us prepare our families. Let us prepare our churches. We must be ready for the greatest opportunity of Christian ministry ever in the history of the church. These days are *omega* days. We need an Omega Church to reach forth into these special days.

Rather than speak generally of the preparation of the Omega "end times" Church, I will use a specific example—an Omega Church in Southern California. Although some of the preparations and developments of this particular body are unique to it and its area, its example will serve as a guideline.

Ministry to the Table

In this church the *Share Table* is a daily, mostly Sunday, sharing experience for the whole body. A long, hand-hewn table of California redwood is situated just inside the church entrance. Food and small personal and household items are placed there as people come into a service. Many times the table is laden with homemade jelly, jam, pickles, bread, and cookies. Often a special sale item from a local supermarket will show up here. Small appliances such as hair dryers, razors, and kitchen mixers find their way to the long table. During garden season, produce is piled high for all to share. The Share Table is not really for those who need food in quantity, but is for everyone in the fellowship that all may experience the joy of sharing.

The *Pantry* is specifically for food ministry to those who are in need of groceries. The Pantry contains quantities of dried food and staples such as beans, rice, and flour, as well as a variety of canned goods. It is stocked with food the fellowship purchased wholesale, food brought in on Pantry Day, and ten percent of all that is canned and preserved from the church garden. No "fluff" or junk foods are stored in the Pantry.

If those in need are not born again, then the salvation message as well as groceries is shared with them. Special paper sacks with printed Scriptures of God's provision and love are used to sack up Pantry groceries. Relevant and inspirational tracts and books are also put in the bags. A group of ladies of the church are responsible for the Pantry, and have divided the work into the two categories of supply and distribution.

The church garden is located on a large ranch owned by the church. The "Green Thumbers," a group of church men, are responsible for the heavy work of plowing, soil preparation, and irrigation. They also have general oversight of the garden from preparation and planting to harvest. When special planting, weeding, and harvest days are announced, members of the fellowship go out to the garden to work.

Plantings are fun for the whole family. Under the guidance of the Green Thumbers, families have been planting garden seeds at home in egg cartons, boxes, and garden flats. The seeds are sprouted and attain first growth at home and then are transplanted into the garden. The garden gets a head start, and each family gains a feeling of responsibility for the garden.

As the garden is harvested, the produce is canned, shared fresh on the Share Table, and given to those in need. The canned goods go into the Pantry for distribution in ministry as needed. Planting, growing, harvesting, and then distributing food for ministry to those in need is a fulfilling experience. This is especially true for those who live in the city.

Promise Ranch

Promise Ranch is an eighty-acre farm-ranch purchased by this Omega Ministry as a means of fulfilling some of its ministry potential. The farm is equipped to grow hay and grain crops to feed the ranch livestock. A poll of the animals shows a vast variety. There are horses, cows, sheep, goats, pigs, chickens, turkeys, rabbits, and an old burro named "Buster."

Promise Ranch is used as a learning center. Families learn to work together growing their own food. They also get back to basics; some are working with their hands for the first time ever.

The ranch is just two hours' driving time from the church, readily available for many uses, including prayer retreats, special classes, youth and fellowship outings, camps, and community outreach activities. It is a haven for all in the fellowship who want to keep one foot in the simple life.

Clothing and Household Necessities

Often those poor enough to need food are poor in other areas. The *Closet* is a ministry of clothing. Baby clothes, children's clothes, adult coats and jackets are always appreciated. The Closet is supplied by members of the fellow-ship, who bring their good used clothing, cleaned and pressed, to the Closet reception area. The Closet is man-aged by a group of ladies of the church who are deft at clothes repair and maintenance. The clothes are received, sorted, repaired, cleaned, and pressed, if necessary, then put on shelves or hangers in clothing-store fashion.

Only those clothes of the best quality and repair are ac-cepted for the Closet. The rest are sorted out and taken to an agency that receives poorer clothing.

The Closet has a section for babies and new mothers, liberally stocked and chaperoned by the "Grandmothers' Club"—a group dedicated to helping young mothers and babies. They make baby quilts and clothing. They provide service, counsel, and love where and when needed. Two of the most appreciated services are the three-day live-in care for the new baby, and the one-month diaper service.

The *Attic* is a ministry providing living necessities for the household. Furniture, appliances, sheets and blankets, cooking utensils, and household tools are among those things found in the Attic. It is managed by the "Grand-fathers' Club." These are men with both the time and the ability to handle and maintain these items.

Like the Closet, the Attic receives only articles in good repair or needing only minor repair. The Attic is an excel-lent place to put items from the garage that are too good to throw away, but too cumbersome to keep. Unlike the Pan-try, which is mainly a ministry of "outreach," the Attic is mainly a ministry of "inreach." Young married couples and needy families of the fellowship are some of those who will greatly benefit from the Attic. Others of the fellowship with a specific need find the Attic helpful. A young wife had two steam irons. She brought one to the Attic to share. She had been wanting and praying for a kitchen mixer. While at the

Attic, she saw just the mixer she wanted. She left the iron and took home the mixer. This is the caring of common communion.

Homemaking I and II

Many cute little sayings that become all-too-truisms surround the subject of cooks and cooking. Yet, I suppose the humor in the poem of the Earl of Lytton finds a niche next to every husband's stomach:

> We may live without poetry, music and art;
> We may live without conscience, and live without heart;
> We may live without friends; we may live without books;
> But civilized man cannot live without cooks.

The Earl of Lytton (1831–1891) would be rather disappointed if he were "earling" today. Our modern culture has all but eliminated home cooking as a skill of the young homemaker. Prepared foods and food kits have had a devastating effect on the kitchen dignity and ability of today's housewife. She has become a one- or two-dish cook. She has studiously mastered chicken *tetrazzini*, but her fried potatoes have Frisbee potential. Perhaps her chocolate mousse is the pride of the neighborhood, but her meat loaf would be declared "beyond grace" at the rescue mission.

One young housewife thought she had the answer to her problem. She got a job. Monday night she and her husband ate chicken with the Colonel. Tuesday was hamburgers under the Golden Arches, Wednesday was Chinese food at Ling Chow's, while Thursday was sirloin at Mr. Steak's. Friday night was spent in the line at the Swedish smorgasbord. Saturday was at-home night, with pizza sent in by Mr. Pizza. Sunday was home cooking—at her mother's! Her take-home pay from her new job was just about the cost of food and gas!

As homemaking is part of our Christian heritage and responsibility, the entire sisterhood of the church is involved in classes on cooking, preserving, and sewing, all taught on a regular basis. Baking and canning projects punctuate the program.

Four times a year all-day and evening sessions with the back-to-basics theme are held. During the holiday season, special cooking is done by the ladies and displayed and shared on the Share Table. Teenagers are given home projects that extend their cooking experience. Cakes and cookies from these projects are used by the church hostess as gifts of love for shut-ins.

Sewing is a very important and popular homemaking project. New machines, methods, and materials make it exciting even for the young.

Not only mothers but teenagers, too, make many of their own clothes. Once a year a dinner is held where clothing made and modeled by the sisterhood is presented. This event is sponsored by the "Seamsters," the senior women of the fellowship. The "Buttons and Bows," the youthful stitchers, sponsor a yearly luncheon where they, too, show their creations. The church has purchased sewing machines that stay right in the classroom. Some older machines given to the church are used as loaners to people needing to borrow a machine. Seamsters are always on the lookout for bargain materials and sales.

Homemaking is also for the men. Classes on home repair, first aid, and family finance are taught by members of the brotherhood and sisterhood, and are offered as coeducational. Singles as well as couples are urged to attend.

Trouble Teams

"A trouble is a trouble, and the general idea, in the country, is to treat it as such." William McFee was right on in his understanding of how to treat trouble. We could add, though, that in the city, as in the country, we must treat it as such.

A psychiatrist once said that the only action one could take when in trouble was "to fight, to flight, or make a deal." Aside from any possible conclusions here, there is a better approach. Christians are to prepare themselves and their circumstances for times of trouble so that they can face it courageously and victoriously. They must not only face it themselves but be able to minister to others at the same time. Jesus told us in Matthew 24 that trouble would come but that we were not to be troubled. Matthew 24 was written that we might prepare ourselves against the time of trouble. He wants us to be the victors, not the victims. The Omega Church is to be prepared to minister in times of trouble, to stand ready to help in days of disaster.

Personal Disaster. There are three areas of personal disaster in which the church can stand ready to help. They are physical, financial, and social.

Physical disaster can take many forms, but the most cruel is injury to life and limb. Injuries are varied, as are circumstances, so help and assistance must be just as varied. Help might mean actual physical help. It could mean money for a hospital bill, or blood from the Omega Blood Bank.

When a young, crippled girl could not come to church because she had no help to get herself and her wheelchair to Sunday services, a trouble-team member began to pick her up Sundays in his van. Another member cares for her while at church.

When a young mother was very pregnant with her second child and the time came for her to deliver, the hospital would not accept her. A trouble-team member went to the hospital, paid a portion of the bill, and made arrangements for the couple to pay the rest. The hospital accepted the arrangements with the backing of the church. The Grandmothers' Club got right on this case and gave the young couple so much TLC that they won them both to the Lord.

When a young, divorced mother of the fellowship gave birth to twins, she needed five pints of blood. The blood was given, but the cost was enormous for her modest income. A trouble-team member called the Omega Blood Bank, and the blood was replaced free of charge. (If the blood bank had not been planned and prepared, no blood would have been available.)

Not every personal disaster can be aided by the trouble team. Sometimes the problem is too vast, or too complicated, and sometimes too many happen at one time to handle them all. But to the glory of God, many are helped in a substantial way that also results in a spiritual blessing for them and the church.

The Omega Church has three trouble teams. Each team is headed by a "ministry elder." (There are ministry elders and ministry deacons in the church.) The first trouble team is named AHIEZER—*brother of help*. The second trouble team is AHISAMACH—*brother of support*. The third trouble team is called AHINADAB—*liberal brother*. The teams are given Bible names because they have Bible meanings and Bible missions. The names are just cryptic enough to be inoffensive and are gleefully referred to by the congregation as "The Triple A."

Natural Disasters. In early 1976, Guatemala was literally devastated by a killer earthquake. In its first few minutes, thousands were killed. Whole towns were destroyed. Countless thousands were injured. All food and water supplies were cut off. Communications were limited to a few ham-radio operators. Government agencies were un-

prepared for the totality of destruction and widespread
need.

An organization that was ready to go into action, though,
was CEPA (English translation: Committee for Emergency
Aid), an evangelical Christian organization that had been
formed and prepared for this very purpose. Trained Christians put on their CEPA armbands and began to set up
medical stations and food kitchens. Martial law was in effect, and looters were shot on sight. No one was allowed to
move about the country. Yet, Christians wearing CEPA
armbands could move freely and minister as they pleased.
Much of the food and supplies flown into Guatemala was
received and distributed by CEPA. A conservative estimate
is that thousands of lives were saved, and many more thousands found Christ as Saviour in Guatemala after the
earthquake because some Christians called CEPA were
prepared for a natural disaster.

The Omega Church must be ready to aid and to minister
in times of natural disaster. Whether it be in earthquake-
prone California, the tornado alley of the Midwest, or the
states that battle the wind and water of hurricane and flood,
we must be ready.

But don't state and federal agencies handle this kind of
thing? Yes, in normal times they do, but these are not normal times, nor are they likely ever to return to normal.
Long-range meteorologists, as well as the Bible, prophesy
strange and vicious weather patterns. Earthquake forecasts
are becoming more accurate and factual, and scientists are
predicting big ones.

The church of the last days must be prepared to give aid
and comfort, both physically and spiritually, to victims of
natural disasters. Churches are most unprepared in the
physical area.

Our Southern California church example, however, is

prepared for natural disasters. It has planned for and is prepared to:

(1) Turn its buildings into aid stations
(2) Utilize its Red Cross blood bank
(3) Distribute food
(4) Purify and dispense water
(5) Disperse field-trained first-aid teams
(6) Take in the homeless
(7) Mobilize ham- and CB-radio teams for emergency communications.

The Omega Church has spiritual-aid-and-comfort plans, as well. In times of great physical stress, people are often in emotional, mental, and spiritual distress. This is an excellent time to present the claims of Christ as Saviour, Physician, and Comforter. The church's spiritual plan is as follows:

(1) To manifest love, joy, and peace in every endeavor
(2) To have each member's home become a spiritual-aid station
(3) To witness actively the saving grace of God to all who will listen
(4) To distribute preprinted tracts and booklets with the theme of salvation, strength, and comfort
(5) To provide Bibles for all who make decisions
(6) To minister healing in the name of Jesus
(7) To establish a twenty-four-hour prayer chain for the duration

Spiritual Training

The goal for the spiritual training of an Omega Church member is simple, systematic, and salvation centered. It is to make every member a student, every member a teacher, and every member an evangelist.

To make every member a student, the Bible is the text. To gain the knowledge of its contents is our desire. We are reminded here of A. Edward Newton's scholastic conclusion from *A Magnificent Farce:* "From contemplation one may become wise, but knowledge comes only from study." There is nothing like that glowing mix of inspiration and perspiration called study to acquaint us with the proclaimed truths of God's Word.

The Omega Church has built much of its preparation around the teaching ministry of the Bible. Home Bible studies supplement regular weekly studies at church. Cassette recordings of Bible studies are available for individual Bible study.

The step from student to teacher is a large one, yet may be no step at all. That is, some students may never be teachers, but all teachers must remain students. A teacher is not only one who studies but one who does, as well. There is a nagging suspicion in our society that teachers are more talk than walk. George Bernard Shaw summed it up: "He who can, does. He who cannot, teaches." The Christian teacher must be acutely aware of this accusation. The Prophet Ezra lived beyond this problem: "For Ezra had prepared his heart to seek the law of the Lord, and to do it, and to teach in Israel statutes and judgments" (Ezra 7:10). First, Ezra sought or studied the law of the Lord. Then he did the law, and then he taught in Israel.

The Omega Church teaches its members how to be teachers by teaching them first how to be students, and then to live what they learn. This combination of learn and live earns them the right to teach.

The third step of the Omega Church's spiritual goal is that everyone be an evangelist. What is an evangelist? An evangelist is a "bearer of Good News." Every Spirit-filled Christian must bear the Good News that "there is therefore now no condemnation to them which are in Christ Jesus . . ." (Romans 8:1). Every Christian must proclaim that Jesus came "to seek and to save" those who are lost (Luke 19:10). The Great Commission to go into all the world and preach the Gospel was given to each Christian and not just to each preacher. Christians must be the bearer of His Good News as surely as they are the bearers of His name.

The Omega Church has classes in soul winning for all its members. The message from the pulpit constantly sharpens the evangelistic awareness of the people. Tracts and books are available at the Carpenter Shop (the bookstore). Street witnessing and house-to-house sharing are part of the training these evangelists receive. The goal of "every member an evangelist" is obtainable. It has to be. The whole world is waiting!

11

How Should We Then Live?

"How should we then live?" This is the question asked by Francis A. Schaeffer in his book by the same name, which discusses the decline and decay of Western culture. Schaeffer borrows this question from an earlier writer, the Prophet Ezekiel. As Ezekiel, Schaeffer, and I share a common concern, it is fitting for us to share a common chapter theme.

This theme comes from the Watchman passage in Ezekiel 33:1–11, 19. The theme is in verse 10:

> Again the word of the Lord came unto me, saying, Son of man, speak to the children of thy people, and say unto them, When I bring the sword upon a land, if the people of the land take a man of their coasts, and set him for their watchman: If when he seeth the sword come upon the land, he blow the trumpet, and warn the people; Then whosoever heareth the sound of the trumpet, and taketh not warning; if the sword come, and take him away, his blood shall be upon his own head. He heard the sound of the trumpet, and took not warning; his blood shall be

upon him. But he that taketh warning shall deliver his soul. But if the watchman see the sword come, and blow not the trumpet, and the people be not warned; if the sword come, and take any person from among them, he is taken away in his iniquity; but his blood will I require at the watchman's hand. So thou, O son of man, I have set thee a watchman unto the house of Israel; therefore thou shalt hear the word at my mouth, and warn them from me. When I say unto the wicked, O wicked man, thou shalt surely die; if thou dost not speak to warn the wicked from his way, that wicked man shall die in his iniquity; but his blood will I require at thine hand. Nevertheless, if thou warn the wicked of his way to turn from it; if he do not turn from his way, he shall die in his iniquity; but thou hast delivered thy soul. Therefore, O thou son of man, speak unto the house of Israel; Thus ye speak, saying, If our transgressions and our sins be upon us, and we pine away in them, *how should we then live?* (Author's italics.)

Say unto them, As I live, saith the Lord God, I have no pleasure in the death of the wicked; but that the wicked turn from his way and live: turn ye, turn ye from your evil ways; for why will ye die, O house of Israel? . . . But if the wicked turn from his wickedness, and do that which is lawful and right, he shall live thereby.

How should we then live? First, we must consider our condition. Consider that we are in the last days—days in which we find ourselves grotesquely unprepared to cope. We discover that we are more and more dependent on people and things that are less and less dependable. The world around us careens from crisis to crisis. The institution of marriage and the family is under constant siege. Most churches are still searching for their reason for being, and finding none. The impotence of organized good is no match for the arrogance and cruelty of organized evil.

Time to Change

The consideration of these circumstances brings us to
Matthew, chapter 24, where two thousand years ago these
troublous times were prophetically penned. At that time it
was prophesied that "these things must come to pass"
(verse 6). It was then quickly added, "But the end is not
yet." There is time for preparation. There is time for
change.

We must change our attitudes and we must change our
life-styles. By changing the way we live to coincide with the
mind of Christ (*see* Philippians 2:5; 1 Corinthians 2:16) and
the life of Christ (*see* Matthew 11:29; Ephesians 1:4), we
can be in preparation for these last days. Our attitudes determine our activity. If we respond to the stimuli of a world
that is depraved and deteriorating, we will activate deprav-
ity and deterioration in our lives.

The need for the renewed mind that Paul speaks of in
Romans 12:2 was never more urgent than it is today. The
text gives the purpose of the renewed mind as proving
"what is that good, and acceptable, and perfect, will of
God." It is a spiritual process that enables us to break our
worldly "mind set," and become good stewards of a Christ-
like mind. The kind of wholesome, godly mind is outlined in
Philippians 4:8:

> Finally, brethren, whatsoever things are true, what-
> soever things are honest, whatsoever things are just,
> whatsoever things are pure, whatsoever things are
> lovely, whatsoever things are of good report; if there be
> any virtue, and if there be any praise, think on these
> things.

When we have changed our mind attitudes, we become
eligible to change our life-styles. As children of the superin-

dustrial technosociety, we find ourselves in the unenviable position of altering a style of life that is so complex and confusing, it defies comprehension, let alone change. What a contrast to the close-to-the-land, close-to-the-people life manner of Jesus. He was never under the tyranny of the urgent. Therefore, He had time for the important. Our lives must exhibit the holiness and discernment of the quiet Christ. We, too, must choose the important over the urgent, the simple over the complex, the person over the project. To effect this kind of change, we must employ the dynamic, changing power of the Holy Spirit—not to change us intrinsically only, as He did at conversion, but to alter the extrinsic, also. Our postconversion life-style, this cultural Babylonism, must be changed! We must now live in every respect as "children of light" (Luke 16:8).

Paul's declaration to us is:

> But of the times and the seasons, brethren, ye have no need that I write unto you. For yourselves know perfectly that the day of the Lord so cometh as a thief in the night. For when they shall say, Peace and safety; then sudden destruction cometh upon them, as travail upon a woman with child; and they shall not escape. But ye, brethren, are not in darkness, that that day should overtake you as a thief. Ye are all the children of light, and the children of the day: we are not of the night, nor of darkness. Therefore let us not sleep, as do others; but let us watch and be sober. For they that sleep sleep in the night; and they that be drunken are drunken in the night. But let us, who are of the day, be sober, putting on the breastplate of faith and love; and for an helmet, the hope of salvation. For God hath not appointed us to wrath, but to obtain salvation by our Lord Jesus Christ.
>
> 1 THESSALONIANS 5:1–9

Just Imagine!

Once we have changed our manner of thinking and living to coincide with that of the crucified Christ, we are ready to join forces with the universal body of Christ in a concerted effort to reach out to the world. This can only happen as the body of Christ (the church) leaves the arena of conflict and the field of competition, and enters the halls of cooperation.

Can you imagine what would happen if the churches and the parachurch groups that make up the organized body of Christ unified in one great thrust to win the world for God? What would happen if all competition and conflict were to cease, and coalition and cooperation were to take their place? It is difficult for us even to begin to comprehend the fullness of this.

Yet, this is exactly what we must do to fulfill the prayer of Jesus Christ in John 17:21–23:

> That they all may be one; as thou, Father, art in me, and I in thee, that they also may be one in us: that the world may believe that thou hast sent me. And the glory which thou gavest me I have given them; that they may be one, even as we are one: I in them, and thou in me, that they may be made perfect in one; and that the world may know that thou hast sent me, and hast loved them, as thou hast loved me.

We are to be one in every vital respect even as God the Father and God the Son are one. This is of essential importance in the task of evangelizing the world, for this unity is a necessary precedent "that the world may believe that thou hast sent me" (John 17:21). We must have unity in order that *the world may believe*. We also must conclude that an unbelieving world exists in direct ratio and proportion to a church that is in dissension and disunity. We must lay aside the cudgels of conflict and pick up the chalice of communion. Let us be one that the world may be won!

To accomplish this will take total commitment, to God and to each other. Complete dedication is our only course of action. The commitment that God requires of us in our relationship with Him is so total and complete that it inherently includes our commitment to each other. Our relationship with the Creator presupposes a commensurate relationship with His creation.

This God kind of commitment involves two stages of life dedication as outlined for us in Psalms 37:5: "Commit thy way unto the Lord; trust also in him; and he shall bring it to pass."

Our first stage of commitment is initial and has to do with decision. We first of all must decide to live a committed life. The second stage is continuation, and has to do with deportment. Once we have decided to live a committed life, we must then daily perform the promise of that decision. This "dailiness" is more difficult than the initial decision. The first stage of commitment is based on faith. The second stage is based on trust.

The Christian who finds it difficult to trust or commit himself to other Christians is usually lacking in second-stage commitment to God. We must trust God to be able to trust each other.

As we trust God and each other, we only then can move into perfect communion. There is a heavenly joy that accompanies this communion that can only be described as celebration. Let us be happy and joyful as we work and worship and win together, "for the joy of the Lord is our strength!" (*See* Nehemiah 8:10.)

These last days must witness our best devotion. The last
letter of the message in God's alphabet is written upon the
walls of the world. These *omega* days demand *omega*
deeds. Let us join with John Milton as he exclaims:

> See golden days, fruitful of golden deeds
> With Joy and Love triumphing.